What you have in your hands is  cigars available in the world! You r<u>e</u> **You simply must have it.** Here's a

First of all, if you are at all ser.... about cigars, **this book will save you more in a month than your CPA saved you in taxes last year**. And <u>not</u> by smoking "low end" cigars, either!

Want more? How about a book so humorously written that you **will positively laugh your ash off from beginning to end**! And just chock-full of shrewd information on every aspect of the cigar hobby. **You'll learn**:

✓ what makes a good cigar, ✓ where to find them,
✓ how to smoke them, ✓ what to pay for them,
✓ how to store them, ✓ how to handle them,
✓ how to fix them, ✓ what toys go with them,
✓ how to find out even more about them and much more.

But don't just take our word for it. Have a look at **what other cigar insiders are saying about the book**. Then check out the brief *Introduction - Why YOU Must Have This Book!* on page 13. You'll see why you <u>really are going to love</u> **The Sensible Cigar Connoisseur**.

> "This is really my kind of book - irreverent, funny, and full of wisdom ... this book will be around for a long, long, time. I just can't believe this son-of-a-gun beat me to writing it!"
> **--Lew Rothman, President and CEO, J.R. CIGAR**

> "Even I learned a few things ... Could not put it down ... You'll see stacks of this one next to the cigars at Tobacco Village."
> **--Sandra Pellot, Owner, Tobacco Village**

> "Dr. Camarda's new book is the perfect complement to the bull market in cigars. No irrational exuberance here. Just hard, lean, value-school advice. Read it! It will take you to new heights of cigar-smoking pleasure. "
> **--Tim Buchanan, Stockbroker**

the

Sensible

CIGAR

Connoisseur

A keen and irreverent look at how to make the most
of one of life's richest pleasures.

While laughing all the way, cigar after cigar.

Required reading for all Cigar Masters!

Jeff Camarda, CFP, Ph.D.

FRANKLIN MULTIMEDIA
O R A N G E   P A R K

a
BrainWare
book

A **BrainWare** Book

Printed in the United States of America

FIRST EDITION

05 04 03 02 01 00 99 98   10 9 8 7 6 5 4 3 2 1

Published in the United States of America by Franklin Multimedia, Inc.

Grateful acknowledgment is made to the following:
Editor: Carrie Beasley Jones, Rene Wilke
Cover Photography: Jim Abrisch, Carriage House Studios
Cover Design: Deric Pearce
Director Marketing Development: Clifford J. Camarda
Cover Model: Kimberly D. Cumming

Publisher's Cataloging-In-Publication
(Provided by Quality Books Inc.)
Camarda, Jeff.
   The sensible cigar connoisseur : a keen and irreverent
look at how to make the most of one of life's richest
pleasures : while laughing all the way, cigar after cigar
/ Jeff Camarda. -- 1st ed.
   p. cm.
   "Required reading for all cigar masters!"
   Includes index.
   LCCN: 98-86586
   ISBN: 0-9665495-7-0

   1. Cigars--Social aspects. 2. Cigars--Humor. I.
Title.

GT3020.C36 1999   394.1'4
                             QBI98-976

FRANKLIN MULTIMEDIA
J A C K S O N V I L L E
418 Kingsley Avenue, Orange Park, FL 32073

Table of Contents

INTRODUCTION: WHY YOU MUST HAVE THIS BOOK! ... 13

FOREWARD BY LEW ROTHMAN 29

CHAPTER ONE: THE JOY OF SMOKE

One Of Life's Great Pleasures.................................... 37
The Purpose Of This Book 38
Becoming A Shrewd Smoker 38
The Brightest Days Of The Cigar Hobby 40

CHAPTER TWO: CIGARS AND HEALTH

What The Life Insurance Industry Says 43
Safest Form Of Tobacco Use 45
Health & Smoking Safety 46
    Safety Tips 46
    Moderation 48

CHAPTER THREE: THE BASICS OF THE BEAST

The Cigar Spectrum 49
Cigar Construction 51
    Every One Is Different 51
    How Cigars Are Rolled 52
    The Inevitable "Bad" Cigars 53
    The Cigar's Guts: Pick Them With Care 53
    What "Hand Made" Really Means 55
    Same Brand, Different Country:
        Yes, We Have No Habanas 56
    A Note On Brands.. 57
    The Ideal Cigar Draw 59

Categories of Quality: Super Premium to the
Bundle In The Bag 60
The Super-Premium 61
Premium Cigars 63
Brand Cigars 64
Bundle Cigars 66

Chapter Four: A Cigar's Finer Points...
The Beauty Of The Beast

Cigar Anatomy 71
Binder 71
Blend 72
Wrapper 73
Colors 75
Shape And Why Size Matters 77
Unusual Shapes 79
The Thickness Makes The Difference 79
Standard Shapes 80

Chapter Five: Cigar Countries...
The Lair Of The Beast

Why Country Of Origin Is Now Less Important 85
The Four Jaguars 87
Cuba 87
Dominican Republic 89
Honduras 89
Nicaragua 90
Jaguar Kittens, a Canary, and Tigers, Too! 91
Mexico 91
Jamaica 91
Philippines 92
Canary Islands 92
Brazil 92
China 92
Columbia! 93

CHAPTER SIX: WHERE TO FIND 'EM, HOW TO BUY 'EM RIGHT

Traditional Sources 95
    Tobacconists 95
    Mail Order Houses 98
    Drugstores 101
    Liquor Stores 102
    Strategies For A Tight Market 102
The Man On The Street: le Count de Counter-feet .. 104
    Spotting Counterfeits 105
Cigar Clubs, Bars, and Restaurants:
    The Call of the Big Smoke 106
Buying Abroad (or two) 108
    A Breath of Fresh Smoke 108
    Bringing Cuban Cigars Into the U.S. 109

CHAPTER SEVEN: SMOKING MECHANICS AND OTHER RITUALS, CIGAR ETIQUETTE, AND THE FIRST BATCH OF TOYS

The Snobbery of Proper Technique 111
Clipping the Head 112
Cigar Cutters 112
    Guillotine 112
    Cigar Scissors 113
    The V Cut 114
    The Punch 114
    Teeth 115
We Have Ignition! Lighting Do's and Don'ts,
    Or Flaming With Style 116
    The Right Flame 116
    Torching It Off, Or Proper Application
        of the Flame 116
Band Management 117
The Refined Art of Civilized Puffing 118
Relighting An Ignored Cigar, And
    Other Sad Tales 119

A Cigar's Life Span, Ashing, And The
    Kind Act Of Extinguishment 120
  How Long To Smoke 120
  Proper Ashing Technique 120
  Putting It Out And Disposing Of The Corpse 121
Smoking Etiquette 122

CHAPTER EIGHT: CIGAR REPAIRS YOU CAN MAKE IN YOUR BATHROOM

Tools 125
The Plugged Cigar 126
The Uneven Burn 128
The Leaky Wrapper 128
When Worms Strike 129
  Bill's Tale Of The Mouse In The Cigar. 129

CHAPTER NINE: PERFECT STORAGE, AND BIG, WONDERFUL HUMIDORS YOU CAN BUY FOR A SONG

The Ideal Conditions For Robust Health 133
  Devices To Monitor The Ideal Conditions 134
  How To Maintain The Ideal Conditions 135
  Temporary Storage And Old Man Winter 136
  On Age And Aging 138
  The Inevitability Of Marriage 139
The Wide World Of Humidors 140
  Those Finely Crafted Dearly Vended Boxes 140
  Cedar: the Cigar's Friend 141
  An Elegant, Expansive, And Brilliantly
    Cost Effective Alternative 141
  Humidors For The Truly Cheap 142

CHAPTER TEN: THE REST OF THE TOYS

Ashtrays 145
Lighters, And Matches to Be Proud Of 147

Jewelry 149
Holders 150
Smoke Filters For The Air 151
Collectibles 152

CHAPTER ELEVEN: CIGAR RELATED
PERIODICALS AND BOOKS

Magazines 155
    Cigar Aficionado 155
    Smoke 156
Cigar Books Worth A Puff Or Two 156
    The Ultimate Cigar Book 157
    Nat Sherman's A Passion For Cigars 158
    The Cigar Companion: A Connoisseur's Guide .. 158
    Leads From An Electronic Bookstore 159

CHAPTER TWELVE: SMOKIN' UP THE WORLD WIDE WEB

Magazine Sites 166
    Cigar Aficionado 166
    SMOKE 167
Other Commercial Launch Points 167
    The Tobacconist 167
    Columbia Unversity Cigar Society 168
    The Internet Cigar Group 168
    Fujipub.com Cigar Page 169
    Whizstreet "Up in Smoke" Cigar Band
        Museum Cigar Links 170
Cigar Radio 171
    Smoke This!!! 171
    Lighten Up! Cigar Radio Network 172

CHAPTER THIRTEEN: DR. CAMARDA'S FAVORITE BRANDS

Punch and Hoyo de Monterrey 173
Bances 174
Excalibur 174
J.R. Ultimates 174

Baccarat 175
Joya De Nicaragua 175
Mocha 175
Nameless Honduran and Nicaraguan Bundles 176
Cuban Partagas, Punch, and Hoyo de Monterrey 176
Dominican Partagas 176
A. Fuente 177
Don Mateo 177
Favorite Sizes.. 177
Favorite Colors.. 178
Final Warning!.. 178

CHAPTER FOURTEEN: STRICTLY FOR WOMEN

Cigar Smoking Tips for Women 180
    Cigar Selection for Women 180
    Preparing the Cigar to Smoke 182
    Actually Smoking the Darn Thing...................... 183
    On Teasing Men with Your Cigar 184
Selecting Cigars for Men 184

CHAPTER FIFTEEN: DR. CAMARDA'S FAVORITE SPIRITS
AND OTHER CIGAR BEVERAGES

Coffee 187
Beer 188
Wine.. 189
Whiskey 190
Rum 191
Cordials 191
Manhattan Special 191

CHAPTER SIXTEEN: THE TRUE-CIGAR MASTER'S
TRIAL-BY-SMOKE TEST 193

EPILOUGE: TO BOLDLY SMOKE WHERE NO BEING
HAS SMOKED BEFORE 201

ABOUT THE AUTHOR 203

APPENDIX: AN INDUSTRY ON FIRE:
          CIGAR SALES AND GROWTH STATISTICS
An Industry on Fire 211
National Cigar Sales Data 212
Cigar Aficionado Circulation Data 214
Smokin' Stocks 214

INDEX 219

Why YOU Must Have This Book!

You are going to love this book!
You must have it!

Hi, I'm Dr. Jeff Camarda. What you have in your hands is simply <u>the best book on cigars available in the world</u>! You really are going to love it. <u>You must have it</u>. Here's a quick preview why:

First of all, if you are at all serious about cigars, **this book will save you more in a month than your CPA saved you in taxes last year**. I don't mean by smoking supermarket cigars. I mean by **getting the same or better cigars for as little as a tenth of what you're now paying**. Right where you usually buy your cigars! <u>And your tobacconist will be happy to help you. They don't like overpaying for cigars any more than you do.</u>

Want more? How about a book so humorously written that you **will positively laugh your ash off from beginning to end**!

And featuring **Florida's hottest model on the cover**, smokin' - in the most dignified and alluring way - just for you. But you knew that already.

Perfect for new and intermediate cigar lovers. A gift for which you will be thanked many times. And just **chock-full of uproarious information** that will **teach even the most seasoned stogie more than a few things**.

Just look at all you get:

Like what countries, sizes, and colors are best, and why • What you really need to know about cigars and health • How to inspect a cigar to tell if it is good before you buy it • How to get Cubans if you want 'em • Spotting counterfeits • How to buy the best for pennies • What "hand made" really means • Why size matters • All about all the toys and where to find them • A stogie-surfer's guide to the Internet • What to look for in construction • Where to get them, how to but them right • Complete cradle (lighter) to grave (ashtray, or neighbor's lawn) cigar care • How to fix cigars in your own bathroom using the tools you got for Christmas • Where to find a prince's sleep-in mahogany humidor for under $100 • Humidors for the truly, truly cheap • What about smoke filters? Cigar collectibles • Cigar music! (would you believe it?) How to keep 'em humidor fresh wherever you go The best ways to remove the head • About the other cigar books (one or two of which you should have...but only one or two) Where to find cigar radio in your city, for gosh sakes • Which old-line brands are best What to drink when you smoke • Traveling with cigars • And much, much more!

And, most importantly, how to find and buy better cigars than you're smoking now, for under a buck...or less...RIGHT HERE, UNDER YOUR NOSE!

This book will take you from wherever you are to **full-CIGAR-MASTER** ...and amuse you so thoroughly that you will weep that there is no more when you are finished!

In a moment I will tell you why this is so. **But don't take my word. Have a look at what others have said.** And believe me, these folks are in a position to know.

Rave Reviews for The Sensible Cigar Connoisseur

"This is really my kind of book - irreverent, funny, and full of the wisdom that comes only from smoking cigars for a very long time. Camarda gets it right on - and is about the only author who hasn't been taken in by the false lure of the overpriced super premium. Not only does this guy show you how to find top quality, hand made cigars at 1985 prices, he tells you where to find them, how to keep them, even how to use all the toys that go with them. Plus what the different colors and countries mean to taste, what to avoid, why size matters, even how to repair a leaky, torn wrapper or cigar with a too-tight draw. Plus he reviews all the magazines and cigar sites on the Web. Without question, this book will help you find the best cigars for your tastes - at rock-bottom prices. Continue to experiment in the wilderness on your own - or save the cost of the book on the purchase of your next two cigars. Keep looking for scraps of knowledge in the slick magazines - or become a cigar-master in your own right, all while laughing your ash off and saving enough on your smokes to retire five years early. It's up to you. Beginner and "old stogie" alike, all will find something to learn here, and an awful lot to smile about. Take it home and enjoy it - unlike a lot of today's cigar hype, this book will be around for a long, long, time. I just can't believe this son-of-a-gun beat me to writing it!"

Lew Rothman, President and CEO
J.R. CIGAR, world's largest seller of fine cigars

"This book is just fantastic! I've been in the cigar business a long time and sold my share of cigar books. This is the only one that pulls it all together. Shows you everything you need to know - including the "insider" stuff you just can't get in the slick magazines. With none of the boring stuff about tobacco fields. And it really made me laugh out loud, all the way through. The book is so good, I just can't keep enough copies in my shop! Wish I'd had it 20 years ago..."

Sandy Jones-Hinton, Owner
Edward's Pipe & Tobacco - San Marco

"Dr. Camarda's new book is the perfect complement to the bull market in cigars. No irrational exuberance <u>here</u>. Just hard, lean, value-school advice. Read it! It <u>will</u> take you to new highs of cigar-smoking pleasure. "

Tim Buchanan, Stockbroker

"...would take years to acquire the...quality information contained in these pages...unique flair for humor...reading extremely enjoyable...this is it!...a must buy...will pay for itself..."

Michael Turber, President
America's Best Cutlery (www.abc-direct.com)

"I love a good cigar almost as much as I love a good deduction...and I <u>love</u> a good deduction! If you love fine cigars as much as I do, this book could save you enough to put your kids through medical school! Smoke like a millionaire for next to nothing. And only your CPA will know..."

Tom Williams, CPA

"Dr. Camarda has hit a home run! This is a humorous, in-depth and wonderful perspective on the fine art of enjoying cigars. It has something for everyone, from the novice to the connoisseur. This book is as rich, robust and hearty as the cigars he smokes. It is a 'must have' for anyone who is interested in this pasttime. My hat is off to Camarda for compiling fantastic reading material for a subject that has eluded truly excellent treatment for far too long."

Daniel R. Mills, Exxon

"If ever there were a financial guru to the cigar world, Camarda is it. I could not believe it was still possible to go out and 'steal' great cigars for under a buck...until I did it! Thanks!"

Dr. Ray Silbar

"Even I learned a few things...Could not put it down...You'll see stacks of this one next to the cigars at Tobacco Village."

Sandra Pellot, Owner
Tobacco Village

"The book is sly, witty, divinely-informed, and funny as hell. Recommended without reserve."

Dr. John Perkins,

This book will teach you more about buying and enjoying cigars in a few hours than a lifetime of reading the slick magazines...buy it"

Kevin O'Grady, Estate Planner

"Yes, this is the cigar book! It will make you a CIGAR-MASTER! You must read it!"

Billy Fraiser
World-Class Bodybuilder and Health Club Owner
(author's note: this guy's been featured on the front page of the Wall Street Journal).

OK. Let's get to my own personal propaganda.

Why This Book is The Best On Cigars Yet and Will Lead The Field For Years To Come

This is a bold statement and I do not mean to be immodest. But consider...

To begin with, there is a dearth of good books on the subject of cigars. Almost none to be found. Oh, there are a handful of titles, but most boil down to "catalog"-type books, full of little more than descriptions of cigar brands, nearly all of which you won't be able to find, or which will have changed dramatically by the time you read the book. Cigar brands do change, quickly, these days. You know they do.

Of the one or two books that give more than that, all spend too many pages on things I bet you don't care about, like tobacco cultivation, tobacco history, recipes, pictures of plants, that sort of thing. <u>Plus they leave a lot of important stuff out</u>, like buying great cigars for under a buck, getting world-class humidors for $50, cigar repair, how to bite the end off like Clint Eastwood (and still be able to smoke the thing), how to make a woman happy with your cigar...I could go on and on.

OK, I made that part up about pleasing woman with cigars (though we <u>do</u> have an entire chapter on cigars for woman, which may prove useful, or at least make you smile). Which brings up the most important thing the two or three other halfway-decent books leave out. The <u>humor</u>.

Yes, **humor**. We're talking about cigars here, not the faded promise of cold fusion or the dilemma of human cloning. <u>Cigars</u>.

Forgive me, but those few other halfway-decent books read as dry and tasteless as sawdust a'sittin' in the sun. Textbook-style. **But don't just take my opinion for it. Look at one. There's probably one sitting right there next to the stack of this one.**

Go ahead, look at it, I'll wait.....................................
....

OK, thanks for coming back. See? I thought you'd feel that way.

On the other hand, **this book will make you <u>howl</u>**. You will laugh, and laugh, and laugh again. **Guaranteed**.

Shucks, I've read some of this stuff thirty times and I still laugh my ash off! And I wrote it, for gosh sakes! I know what's coming. And still I laugh.

And you, my friend, **you will be in stitches**.

You will laugh so hard, you will become a CIGAR-MAS-TER, and not even know you are learning! You will have more fun than you get from your favorite recreational reading...and emerge an expert. In <u>every</u> aspect.

Then you will cry that the book is finished and read it over. And over.

Once again, don't take my word. Read this sample, that I have selected at random by shooting down the WORD file with my mouse. Here goes the mouse! What will we find?

We start out easy, we don't want you clutching your sides with mirth too quickly. We will warm you up.

Here it is, on lighting the cigar:

"You must require a flame burning at precisely 340 degrees Fahrenheit. Any more, and you risk carbonizing the tobacco. Any less, and you get incomplete ignition, and your cigar will knock.

Just kidding, of course, but everyone says butane or a quality wooden match only. Or a bit of smoldering firewood, if you have it handy and are in the mood. Paper matches and lighter-fluid, Zippo-type lighters are no-no's, for the same reason: they produce a flame with nasty-tasting residues which will spoil the taste of a cigar. Paper matches have chemicals in them to help them burn, and lighter fuel is kinda like kerosene. Butane burns clean and whatever flavor wood may impart appears not to be objectionable.

As a practical matter, the smoke from a cigar is slightly more substantial a thing than is, say, the fragrance of a rose and any flavor lent by the bad flames is likely to go unnoticed unless the flame is applied for a peculiarly long time. I avoid paper matches when I can, but notice no real difference when I must use them. I can not remember the last time I used a Zippo - or a burning bolt of magnesium, for that matter - so if these nostalgic lighters appeal to you, you must fire up and judge for yourself.

Car lighters, electric and gas stoves, and gas barbecues are all pretty much OK. Avoid charcoal which has been soaked in starting fluid and burning buildings and vehicles, since these last may contain mixed fuels of unknown type."

Here's another one, on cigar sizes:

"A short, very thin panatela gives us a rakish, Eastwood-esqe look. A longer panatela perhaps gives us a more elegant, continental look. And a larger cigar, say a Churchill, might lend a prosperous (or preposterous), Wall Street, old time Daddy Warbucks sort of style. And while I have learned to consider taste, and nothing more, I still am known to peer in the mirror, cheroot tightly clenched between teeth, on occasion, especially after I've had a tequila or two, and sneer. But I will never forget the words of the lady on the plane. Back in the days when I managed a stock-brokerage branch, returning to Jacksonville after a regional conference, I put a rather large cigar in my mouth just as the plane touched down, in anticipation of getting off. It had been a long flight, and I was tired. A moment later, the lady says, "Well! That cigar's bigger than you are!" To which I innocently replied, with a mock look of bewilderment on my face, after glancing down at my knees for a long moment, "No, it's not." I was able - that time - to turn a rather uncomfortable moment into one of amusement (for all but the well-mannered lady). But know that often, you will be measured by the company of the cigars that you keep."

And another, on the best countries:

"For goodness sake, it looks like the whole world's trying to cash in on the cigar craze. I went surfing last night to develop material for the Cigars on the 'Net chapter and found - would you believe it? - cigars offered from a forgotten valley in Columbia, where they have been made for centuries, which were purported on the Web page to be better even than Cuban Cohibas! At the bargain price of only $140 for the box of 25! And yes! They do take credit cards! Just fax your Mastercard number to our unassuming little, impoverished, druglord-ravaged village, and we will process, with complete security, through the Banco de Bogata! We don't know how long we can keep this up, the bullets are whizzing! And just look at that hand-crafted-by-the- Mayan-pyramids jungle-wood box! Hurry, senor! Ah, they got my brother! You see, my brother dies for your gringo cigars! You better buy some!"

One last bit, from the testing your cigar-mastery-section:
"Totmente a mano," or completely by hand means:
1) A lonely life.
2) The epitome of self-reliance.
3) Just what it says.
4) A pretty good date in high school.
5) Blindness beckons.
6) A fan of the Village People.
The binder:
1) Is impossible to retrieve once the seller has accepted your offer.
2) Is the amount of money you will lose on divorce.
3) Is the thick, heavy part, under the wrapper, which holds the whole thing together.
4) Is the fellow who made this book
To tell real (Cuban) Habanos from the many counterfeits:
1) Insist on a green card for the cigars.
2) Be sure to pay cash.
3) Look for high quality of manufacture and packaging...and smoke one first!
4) Ask the smuggler to show you the "secret code" on the tax stamp."

Enough! We can give no more of this away without some sort of commitment from you! Unless, of course, you insist on flipping through the chapters at your fingertips...
Let's get a bit more serious.

The world of fine cigars is so wide. You newer smokers have a lot to learn, about countries, construction, flavor, and smoking mechanics. And you "old stogies" could learn at very least a thing or two, too. To buy better, buy cheaper, and enjoy the smoke more. And we can all stand to be amused.

As you have noticed, cigars are a complex treat to rival fine wine, and you need to know a few things to enjoy them fully. This book teaches you <u>more</u>, comprehensively, then anywhere else, in a light, humorous style sure to keep you enchanted, and chuckling, from beginning to end.

<u>Perhaps more importantly</u>, the **book shows how to know and find quality product at a bargain price.** Anywhere! It will point the way to the sleepers in the shop you are in <u>right now</u>, or where you go to buy. To pay 75 cents when everyone else pays $5 for a comparable cigar. Not only do <u>we show how, we show where, with details and buying strategies</u>. We give you a treasure map to the humidor!

This no other book does, has even tried. We are also alone in providing a wealth of Internet resources on cigars, and a through review of the related paper literature. And on, and on, and on. Just look at the Table of Contents, to see.

Still not convinced? Here's lots more reasons...

The book is entertaining, truly a joy to read

The information just flows, effortlessly. Nearly every page produces a chuckle or two, and many, many spots cause eruptions of profound laughter. Prolonged laughter. Even on the fifth reading!

For anyone who reads, not just cigar lovers. The humor is sophisticated, spontaneous, and completely appropriate to the subject. We are, again, after all, talking about <u>cigars</u> here, and not world peace.

<u>All</u> of the other books you will see read as dry as the transcript from an actuaries' convention, I think you will find. No one else seems to really try to truly <u>entertain</u> and well as

inform. **Don't you prefer books that are both informative and deeply pleasurable?** This book is both and nothing else on the subject is. **Aren't these the ones you keep on your shelf year after year**, while the others go to the goodwill, or trash, or used-book store? Trust me, **this one's a keeper**. Flip through the chapters if you don't believe me.

We stick to useful topics of interest to today's time-pressed smoker

This book gives you everything you want to know, reads fast, and makes you laugh.

Compare that to what I think is probably the next-best book on cigars.

I tend to be a bit of a scholar, but was bored to tears to plow through <u>that</u> book's endless chapters on tobacco through the ages, and in the fields, despite the fact that his was the first halfway-decent cigar book to find itself into my hands, and I hungered for it. The other books seem to find this stuff obligatory, but I think it is just nonsense to expect a modern smoker to care. About what makes for a good cigar, where to find them, how to smoke them, what to pay, how to store them, how to handle them in public, what toys and drinks compliment them, how to find out more about them, immediately useful stuff like this, **yes!**

About which valleys in Cuba are the most magical to tobacco plants, or where to apply the thermometer in the heap of fermenting wrapper-tobacco to tell when it is done, **no!** Most smokers are unlikely to visit and valley-specific information is awfully hard to come by on a box of cigars. Even if you cared. As far as applying thermometers goes, we probably all got our fill of <u>that</u> in our infancy.

Do you need to know what time is best to cover the tobacco plants with gauze, to give them shade? Do you want to know? We mercifully have not included that kind of stuff in the book.

Not a bit of it.

Ditto for the stuff like the recipes. It may be nice, but I can't remember the last time I whipped up a batch of "death by chocolate cake with strawberries." And I bet most cigar-chomping readers can't, either.

You want a cookbook, or a farmer's almanac?

Or do you instead want a wonderful guide to tell you everything you want to know about cigars, which doesn't waste your time with things you don't want to know, and doesn't spare a word except to make you laugh?

Want to learn to steal great cigars, using the secrets of the pros?

Read on...

We alone give straight information on buying quality cigars at fair prices

This is a serious point. The current craze has spawned a wave of overpriced product, fast-buck artists, and contrived shortages which result in most consumers paying four, five, even ten times what a particular cigar is worth, and can be had for if one knows where and how to look. To quote Lew Rothman, CEO of J.R. Tobacco, the largest cigar seller in the world: "a lot of the cigars today are nothing but real junk in fancy boxes...You see ads in Cigar Aficionado and Smoke Magazine of absolutely gorgeous cigars, along with a bunch of bull**** copy about how some family has been making these things in their basement for a hundred years. Then you run out and end up paying five or ten dollars for a cigar that's almost entirely composed of "green" trash tobacco, wrapped in some mangy Indonesian wrapper...give me a break..."

Lew can be a "tell it like it is" kinda guy, and his point is absolutely dead-on. And you get a full forward from his own pen coming up in the next section. <u>Read it</u>. This fellow is a true god of the cigar universe, having built up a company which dominates the business from next to nothing in just a few decades. It was he who actually said, "let there be smoke."

I suspect he actually <u>owns</u> Costa Rica and parts of Honduras. He also writes a regular column for SMOKE magazine. You will find his insight remarkable. **Nobody else has Lew!**

Good cigars <u>can</u> be had at very reasonable prices: I am at the moment smoking a wonderful, large, handmade, long-filler cigar imported from Honduras, for which I paid about 74 cents. **And you can, too. You can find one right in that humidor over there**.

Many would pay ten times that and be happy! But to paraphrase George Burns: "If I paid that much for a cigar, I'd have to buy it dinner first." And while I didn't have to buy 1,500 of them to get that price (although I did because the value was excellent) - a mere 20 for $16 would have done it - the point is that great cigars can be had very fairly in <u>any</u> quantity desired if one knows what to look for. And we show you <u>how</u>. No one else even <u>tries</u>.

We alone show how to "repair" a damaged or improperly made cigar

While the thought may cause you to snicker, imagine how <u>you</u> would feel if <u>you</u> paid $55 for a Cuban for your last night in some tropical paradise, and found it unsmokable because it was "plugged." Especially if you found out later, after throwing the disloyal beast in the lagoon, how a gentle probe with the right object in the right place could have made it right, and saved the cigar, the evening, and <u>possibly your marriage</u>.

We alone take readers to cigar sites on the World Wide Web

Just about everyone in our targeted reader group is "on line" these days, and has access to the Internet at home or work. As in most things, the Net is rich in cigar related sites - thousands and thousands of places to play and learn in. We give detailed directions to the better sites, with good reviews of the features to be found there. <u>None</u> of the other books even <u>mentions</u> the Internet.

We are alone in giving reviews of paper resources

There are more than a few of cigar related books out there
- even if they are overwhelmingly tangential - and this is the
only book which gives a good listing of them. There may be
one or two worth your attention once you've finished this
one...but which ones for **what you want**? We tell you. No
one else does...maybe they don't want you to know about
the others?

No one. We revel in it. 'Cause once you finish this one,
ain't nothing else gonna come close.

Ditto for the far more important magazines, Cigar Aficionado, and SMOKE. We give detailed reviews along with
subscription information and Internet addresses for the electronic versions. The other books barely mention their exist-
ence. And these magazines changed the face of the industry. We tell you which are best for you, why, and how to
subscribe.

We give far more detailed and useful information on all aspects of the cigar hobby

This book really does cover the entire spectrum of useful
cigar-using tips, from understanding how and what to buy,
to get 25 great cigars for what you now pay for two, down to
such mundane details as how to properly cut one, light one,
put one out, and dispose of it. We cover it all, in thoroughly
entertaining fashion. No one else comes close. Not even
close. Trust me on this...I've read them!

So there you have it!

If you have gotten this far, you are a very careful shop-
per, indeed. My ash is off to you! It has fallen off, watching
you read, and smile!

If you're still not convinced that this is absolutely the
world's best cigar book, that you simply must take it home,
then go get comfy in that wing-chair over there, and read on.

You'll see.

Take all the time you want.

When you leave, I'm confident that you'll walk out with this book tucked under your arm.

Good smoke to you!

Dr. Jeff Camarda
Orange Park, FL
Summer, 1998

P.S. Pssst! Pssssst! The young lady is too polite to mention it, but they're closing! The lights are going out! If you're <u>still</u> not sure, you'll have to come back tomorrow, and ponder some more.

But wouldn't it be so much nicer to take it home and keep reading <u>there</u>?

Just think...this friend-of-a-book in one hand, a fine cigar in the other, your honey bringing you your favorite drink, and smiling mischievously...Ah, bliss!

Foreward by Lew Rothman
Owner and CEO of JR Cigar

"What's Going On in the Premium Cigar Industry?"

Cigars smokers have been plagued by escalating prices and out of stock conditions on their favorite cigars for the last several years, yet the Cigar Manufacturers Association and its member manufacturers and importers report sky-rocketing quantities of premium cigars being produced at factories throughout the Caribbean Basin. It just doesn't make sense. What's the real truth behind this sudden and mysterious shortage?

Is there a real shortage of premium cigars? Is there a shortage of tobacco?

Or...is there a shortage of brains?

It is not a classified government secret that the last few years we have witnessed an incredible rise in the prestige of the connoisseur cigar smoker, the smoker of handmade cigars from the five major cigar producing countries of the Caribbean Basin: Honduras, Nicaragua, Mexico, Jamaica and the Dominican Republic. Nor have consumers of fine cigars been oblivious to the numerous newspaper and magazine articles extolling the renewed popularity of handmade cigars. This re-awakening and attendant publicity to the pleasures of a fine cigar have unleashed forces that have disrupted what was for generations nothing more than a sleepy little industry. It has spawned new consumers, retailers, importers, and manufacturers, all of whom share one thing in common - a lack of knowledge about the products they use, sell, or manufacture. I choose to call these people collectively, "The Cigar Virgins."

During my career in the cigar business, I have come to know many people in the cigar industry and believe that I can honestly speak for most of them when I say that as a group we've never made any "windfall profits" making or selling handmade cigars. The prevailing theory of cigar retailers, importers, and manufacturers alike was always to provide knowledgeable service, quality products, and attractive prices, while still earning a comfortable living. We believed that individual retailers and brands like Punch, Hoyo de Monterey, and H. Upman, etc. Would earn a reputation for providing cigar connoisseurs with superior products which were a true value. We believed our actions would garner the steadfast loyalty of the cigar smoking public and ensure the continued viability of our businesses.

Then came the Cigar Boom, and the Cigar Virgins, and a method doing business which had existed for generations disappeared overnight.

Today, cigar smokers everywhere are routinely being told that the Fuentes or Don Diegos, or other "name brand" cigars that they have smoked and enjoyed for years are out of stock. Instead of obtaining the brands they have grown to know and trust, the consumer is now forced to go home empty handed, or choose from a bewildering array of new "super-premium" cigar brands at ludicrous prices - each of which is touted as being the greatest thing since sliced bread. Where did all these brands come from overnight? Why did it take the cigar industry 200 years to discover how to make a $10 cigar? Where did all the Don Diegos and Fuentes disappear to?

The answers are simple and frightening, wherein simple events caused an unnoticed and unstoppable chain of circumstances leading to radical changes in the premium cigar industry.

Just prior to the rekindling of demand for premium cigars in the United States, and amid growing fears of increasing government regulation of the tobacco industry in the late 1980's and early 90's, non-Cuban cigar manufacturers began an earnest attempt to sell their products to the European Market, long a stronghold of Cuban cigars. Having achieved little or no success in the past, nothing was done to increase cigar production should these attempts prove to be successful, and frankly no one took notice of this first small miscalculation.

However, over a relatively short period of time the large, moist handmade cigars of the type Americans preferred gained consumer loyalty not only in Europe, but in the Near East, Far East, and South Africa as well. And every single cigar that was shipped to these new markets was a cigar that was not shipped to the United States. Then, in 1992 came a startling announcement by Davidoff, a European Tobacco firm, that it would no longer continue to sell Cuban cigars due to what it claimed were inherent problems with the quality of Cuban cigars. Whether the break between Davidoff and Havana was caused by problems of quality or, in reality, by demands on the part of the Cubans to own a controlling interest in the firms which distribute Havana cigars worldwide is another issue, but the event was very significant for two important reasons in adding fuel to the tiny spark which had already been created by the successful distribution of large, American style cigars in Europe.

Davidoff, which operated or licensed a number of stores throughout the world, began to tout Dominican cigars as being superior to the suddenly inferior Cuban cigars, thus adding their stature as Europe's premier cigar dealer to the already growing acceptance of Caribbean Basin cigars, while simultaneously deriding the quality of the Cuban products by announcing the destruction of their existing stocks of Havana cigars rather than offering an inferior product to the public.

Davidoff, divorced from the Havana trade, was now free to enter the American Market where Cuban cigars had been illegal since the Embargo of 1962, and they began to market a new and extraordinarily high priced cigar produced in a factory that had never previously manufactured a successful "name brand" cigar.

These were two momentous happenings which went relatively unnoticed by the cigar industry, but caught the attention of other entrepreneurs. As outsiders, they saw things that the industry failed to see. They realized that the U.S. market was ripe to spend the kind of money Europeans had long been forced to pay for fine cigars, and that cigar importers and retailers were in an excellent position to make some "real money" on the products they sold. Davidoff's move proved that with the proper promotion and packaging Americans would pay dearly for a good cigar. More importantly, it didn't matter who manufactured it.

By late 1993 some slight shortages of "name brand" Premium cigars were starting to be noticed in the United States. Part of these shortages were due to Caribbean Basin cigars being shipped to destinations other than the U.S., and part of the shortage was due to a growing number of Duty Free shops throughout the world who were commencing to explore the money making possibilities of selling large, moist, American style, handmade cigars. BUT- an even greater part of the shortage was caused by entrepreneurs who were contracting with existing manufacturers for "Private Label" cigar brands.

These entrepreneurs, many with no prior experience in the cigar industry, struck deals with a existing cigar manufacturer who was already selling under a "name brand" label. Then, with the addition of some laudatory sales copy regarding the quality of the tobaccos and the expertise of the craftsmen who made this "no name" cigar, they would proceed to market this "new" brand at inordinately inflated prices to retailers throughout the United States as a "super premium" cigar.....and it worked! Cigar retailers, tired of making the traditional 33% profit on cigars selling for a dollar or two were enthralled at the prospect of making 50% on cigars selling for four or five dollars. Simultaneously a fortuitous influx of novice "cigar virgins" drawn into the market by the recent resurgence in the popularity of premium cigars and the advent of an upscale magazine called <u>Cigar Aficionado</u>, seemed more than willing to pay any price to acquire "the Ultimate Cigar."

In 1994, despite increasing cigar production, shortages of handmade cigars began to escalate as Cigar Manufacturers not only diverted part of their production to these private labels, but joined in the private label process themselves. It seemed reasonable that if new entrepreneurs could sell an existing product for a higher price, why couldn't the manufacturers play the same game themselves? BUT, how to do it?

Do they dare take a brand they have sweated and slaved over for decades and summarily raise the price by 100%, and possibly kill the brand? - or would it be safer to take the very same cigar and put it in a new package with a new name? It doesn't take a rocket scientist to guess the answer. Not surprisingly, 1994 saw a tremendous increase in the number of cigar brands being produced and an alarming shortage in the supply of the old time traditional brands...the brands which sold at reasonable prices.

Equally galling to the old line manufacturers was the fact that although they possessed generations of expertise in producing the finest handmade cigars obtainable, new factories and inexperienced novices were not only beginning to compete with the "big guys" for tobacco and labor, but were actually selling their inferior products for vastly higher prices. The big manufacturers reacted by raising workers salaries, and dramatically increasing the prices they were willing to pay for tobacco, all of which unfortunately resulted in an increase in cigar prices which the public was forced to bear.

1995 was a horrible year for the cigar industry, the impact of which will be felt for years to come. Major brands such as Fuente, H.Upman, and Don Diego lost vast segments of their loyal consumers due to absurd shortages of product at traditional tobacconists. It was unbelievable and illogical, BUT, instead of curtailing the number of "Private Label" cigars being produced to stem out of stock conditions and satisfy loyal smokers, the "big guys" made even more new products, making a bad situation worse....and playing right into the hands of all the new "novice" manufacturers.

Veteran cigar smoker in droves were being herded into buying previously unknown cigar brands at insane prices, due to a total and prolonged inability to secure a supply of the very cigars they had routinely purchased for decades. This in turn forced many traditional tobacconists, who had dogmatically shunned these over-priced new "rip-off" cigars, simply because they could obtain nothing else to fill their shelves with as the major manufacturers continued to spread their meager output of name brand products among an ever increasing variety of new outlets which ran the gamut from Wine Shops to the local supermarket.

During 1994 and 1995 the mistakes of the large manufacturers in failing to curtail new products, and failing to supply their traditional tobacconists, inured to the benefit of the little guys, the "buckeyes" as they're called in the industry. Having met with enormous success in selling "no name" products at prices vastly higher than traditional "name brand" cigars, these buckeyes were willing and able to offer significantly higher wages to entice trained cigar makers to leave the big factories. They were also willing and able to offer vastly higher prices for tobacco to feed their fledgling factories.

Today there are yet another round of new faces entering the industry with promises of unlimited cigar supply, but at enormous prices. These are people without the least bit of knowledge about cigars, nor any desire to acquire any. They are charlatans who go about procuring orders from retailers starved for merchandise, then travel to the cigar-producing countries offering fabulous prices to secure merchandise to fill those orders. And those orders will be filled at the expense of less profitable "name brand" products, and tobacco prices, labor, and retail prices will spiral out of control.

Is there really a cigar shortage, or has the production of cigars merely been split up into a bewildering number of cigar brands? The truth of the matter is that the supply of cigars today is greater than it has been in decades, however it is fragmented like a pizza with 80 slices instead of the traditional eight.

Where are all the handmade cigars? Remove them from a thousand wine shops, restaurants and cigar clubs, and put them back where they belong, in the hands of a knowledgeable tobacconist and you'll find the sheer number of cigars is more than adequate.

Why is the brand you've enjoyed for 20 years unavailable? Because a lot more money can be earned by calling it something else.

What does the rest of the Nineties hold in store?

Well, frankly I'm a lot better at commenting on the past than guessing at the future, but my guess is as follows:

Cigar manufacturers are going to wake up one of these days and start using their brains. They can not be so stupid as to ignore the oncoming disaster which awaits the industry if they continue to allow the rapid escalation of prices in tobacco, labor, and cost to the eventual consumer. They can not ignore the raging anger of their consumers caused by unconscionable shortages of name brand cigars on the shelves of genuine tobacco shops. They can not continue to allow the cigar smoking public to be gouged with ridiculously inflated prices simply to demonstrate that their products are the equal of the over-priced "no-name" cigars produced by "no-name" factories.

Our goal here at JR is to find quality cigars for our customers at reasonable prices. Perhaps we won't make as much money as others do on each and every cigar, but we are convinced that over a period of time we will sell most of the cigars in this country. Americans are not stupid. You can fool them once or twice, but sooner or later, quality and common sense will prevail. We intend to be the voice of common sense in an industry that has temporarily gone berserk. When sanity returns to this industry, we will still be here to serve you, while all the charlatans turning out these "no name, super premium cigars" will be gone.

To all you friends out there who have been forced to pay higher prices and wait forever to get your favorite cigars, I tell you just hang in there. Our turn at bat is coming pretty soon, and there's gonna be hell to pay.

Lew Rothman
CEO of 800-JR-CIGAR
Spring 1997 Somewhere in Central America

Author's Post-Foreward

A short post-foreward, I promise. A yard or two, no more.

Just thought I'd tell you a thing or two about Lew to put the forgoing in perspective.

First, he is a brilliant marketer, as demonstrated by the corporate name of his company, "800-JR-CIGAR." When you see it written that way, above and elsewhere in the book, you may think that I am advertising the guy's phone number - and I am sure that was Lew's intent in naming it that way. But this is the company he is president of and I gotta describe it properly.

The second thing about Lew is that he's been in the cigar business forever, and knows not only a heck of a lot about good cigars, but about the industry, as well. It is remarkable how closely his above views parallel my own conclusions, and how accurately what he predicts above has come to pass even in the short time since it was written.

For what it is worth, the company now called "800-JR-CIGAR" is arguably the largest seller of good cigars in the world. It has recently gone public. Lew built it up from his father's candy store in New York City.

And I am honored, indeed, to have him here.

CHAPTER ONE

The Joy of Smoke

"A Woman is just a woman, but a good cigar is a Smoke!"
-- Kipling

"If I cannot smoke in Heaven, then I shall not go."
-- Mark Twain

One Of Life's Great Pleasures

Ah...the joys of a good cigar. Few things in life can bring as much pleasure. And, unlike other of the passions of my youth, this one has not faded with the familiarity of long marriage, or the more subdued desires of middle age. As George Burns said, "the pleasure can go on forever, if you don't inhale." A good cigar is a smoke, indeed.

Of course you agree, if you are reading this. The popularity of our "hobby" has surged tremendously in the '90's, due, in no small part, to the appearance of Cigar Aficionado, a slick, very high-end bi-monthly magazine which for the first time showed the world what many of us had known for awhile - that good cigars are nearly gourmet delights, to be appreciated like fine wines. Cigars have become almost too popular: demand is off the scale, prices for most everything are sky-high, product is hard to find, and poor quality cigars, brightly-banded, and billed as super premiums (though no one has heard their name before) are offered at outrageous prices, and sell too many thousands each day.

The Purpose Of This Book

This book is written as a practical guide to this pastime, written with the beginner in mind, but offering valuable insight to even the most seasoned smoker. By practical, I mean providing information you probably care about, and can put to use right away. Stuff like the qualities that make for a good cigar, why size matters, which countries and wrapper colors are best, where to find and how to spot the best deals, how to store them, all the toys that go with them, and other things like that. Information that most smokers (notice that I didn't say guys, ladies?) will find interesting and usable. I've even included a chapter called "Cigar Repairs You Can Make In Your Bathroom" just in case you tear the wrapper on your $15 Hoyo de all Hoyos, and can't bear to toss it away. What you won't find are some of the things the other cigar books seem to find mandatory, but bore the daylights out of many: stories about the history of tobacco, and the debate over whether the word seegar comes from the Indian (American, or the other kind?), the Cuban, or the Lower East Side. The history and practice of tobacco cultivation. We will spare you the litany of the diseases which can plague the tobacco plant in the field. You won't see any four color photos of the sun setting over Dominican tobacco fields, leaf growing protected under "shade" netting or fermenting to become Maduro wrapper, or even of Cuban woman wielding cigar trimming knives. Well, maybe we'll try to find some photos of Cuban women, but not the other stuff. I'll just try and give you what I think you want, what I would want if I were you.

Becoming A Shrewd Smoker

And it is important, gentle smokers, to arm yourselves with the knowledge to become shrewd smokers. The skyrocket popularity of cigars shows no signs of abating, as more and more people take to the hobby. The "shortages" - which even now are worldwide, by the way, not just confined to the U.S. - will almost surely worsen, as demand further outstrips what the manufacturers can produce. Only so many regions have the climate required to produce quality leaf, after all, and it takes a long time to get new fields into production, before cigars can be rolled and aged.

This means two important things for you. One, the good stuff, the names we know and trust, will be harder and harder to get, vary more in quality, and be more expensive and rationed when you do find it. Two, the rip-off brands will continue to proliferate. The best kind of rip off is the excellent cigar sold at a totally absurd price. Twelve dollars for a Nicaraguan, indeed! Few Cubans are worth that price. As Burns also said, "If I paid that much for a cigar, I'd have to sleep with it first." But the worst kind of rip off, of course, is absolute garbage at a ridiculous price. And you can't tell by the packaging and you can't tell by the name, since new "brands" spring into being almost daily, flaunted in the new catalogs which seem to constantly line our mailboxes. In fact, many of us suspect that more than some of the high priced "new" cigars which are actually good are really output from some of the old, well-loved brands, slapped with a new band and box, so the manufacturer can jack the price for the same product, and still not offend his old, loyal customers, who suffer backorders, and wonder how demand can be so high as to dry up supply. Supply perhaps diverted, perhaps not really dry.

So we will try to help you learn to find what it is you like, then get quality product at fair prices. For those who like "garbage," well and good! I've surely smoked my share. But know what it is and pay what it is worth. But there is good stuff out there, more than has ever before been produced. At this moment I am reveling in a very, very good, hand made, nicely sized Honduran, which cost 65 cents. Yes, Virginia, there are still wonderful cigars to be had for a short song, if you know what to look for, and where to look. We'll show you where to find it, and how to get it at a fair price. But first, we'll show you what it looks like, smells like, and tastes like.

The Brightest Days Of The Cigar Hobby

So enjoy! The world for cigar smokers has never been as bright. And while the majority of the politically correct population still turns up its nose at any sort of smoke (be it from cigarettes, cigars, smokestacks or diesels) cigars now carry a chic, a panache, a mystique that they have not carried for most of the century. Even the PC's among us, while not looking up to cigar smokers, at least do not spit on us as if we were mere cigarette smokers. And that is something, a wonder in just ten years. As a young stockbroker in the mid '80's New York, I was often threatened with violence when smoking in a bar - which gave me pause to consider how effectively a glowing-cigar-enhanced-fist might deliver a retaliatory strike. Strange. As an obnoxious 14 year old in the early '70's I could smoke cheap cigars in drugstores and blow smoke into the faces of patrons with nary a whisper or glance, and ten years later they wanted to shoot me. And now, conditioned by years to cower in shame, when I meekly beg a barkeep that I might smoke, permission is granted with such nonchalance that I can only shake my head in disbelief. Cigars, mind you, in a restaurant, while others are eating! The waiter is surprised that I must ask: "well, sir, you are in the smoking section...." As I write this in the Newark airport, I scurry to the bar (the only smoking section) to have a Heineken and a Honduran. As I light, no one in the crowded room seems to notice except for one woman at the bar, who turns her head and sniffs, nothing more. Victor, the bartender, asks about my cigar and tells me of the box of Cohibas he got through a friend in Dominica. Instead of a tip, I give him one of the bundle Hondurans, which he accepts gladly. As we arrive in the crowded hotel lobby in Venice, another fellow is smoking there before me and no one pays him any mind. And while cigars won't win you any love among teenagers - a recent survey reported that 92% of teenagers said cigars were a big turn off, much higher than the number which felt that body piercing was unattractive...the adult population is clearly finding them more acceptable. You, gentle smoker, have it as never before. You have cigar clubs, smoker nights, and fine restaurants with well stocked humidors next to their wine cellars. You have several quality magazines devoted to the passion, cigar shops, factories, and brands sprouting like weeds, Arnold smoking on planes, Letterman on his show, Madonna with a Churchill between her sculpted ruby lips. The world has changed, in this for the better. Light it up!

CHAPTER TWO

Cigars and Health

Cigars ain't good for you. They can't be. No one rational can believe that wrapping your mucous membranes around the exhaust from a controlled fire can enhance health. At best, they are neutral, benign, make no difference either way. Most likely they are harmful to some degree. But most likely so are sports cars, air travel, lovely members of the sex which most attracts you, and hamburgers. Especially hamburgers with cheese. Risk is relative and perhaps better not to live than to not taste deeply of life. We at best control risk, do not eliminate it. We buy a plane ticket, instead of trying to fly the plane ourselves.

There has been an onslaught in the media lately, timed well to the surging popularity of the cigar smoking hobby. We are warned that cigars cause all manner of illness and perhaps are worse than cigarettes. The studies have been few and far short of comprehensive.

What The Life Insurance Industry Says

It is extremely noteworthy that the life insurance companies have until just very recently considered cigar and pipe smokers the same as non smokers, granting non-smoker and even preferred (offered only to those in the very pink) rates - and let me tell ya, more than a few switched from cigarettes to stogies for a week or two to get the better rates. What this means is that the industry did not consider non-cigarette smoking to significantly alter lifespans: cigar smokers were expected to live about as long as non-smokers, and so did not need to be charged more for their life insurance. This has changed in the past year - though many companies still quote cigar smokers as non-smokers, so look - and most insurance companies now take all " alternative" tobacco use - cigars, pipes, chewing tobacco and snuff - and lump it into the same blackened pot with the infinitely more harmful cigarettes. The official reason for this is that "we are finding cigars more harmful than we thought"; and that giving cigar users non-smoker rates would "encourage something" - smoking in any form - "which we do not support." This is poppycock, according to both common sense, and an extremely accomplished underwriter who spoke at an insurance conference given by one of the companies I represent which now charges cigar users smoker rates. Mortality for cigar smokers is clearly lower than that for cigarette smokers. The real reason for this position, I think, is profit. Higher rates, more drops to the bottom line, all in harmony with political correctness and green Earth. So be it.

This quote from Marv Shanken, editor of Cigar Aficionado, is illuminating:

"The truth seems evident to me. The anti-cigar people are grasping at anything they can find because they don't have concrete evidence to support their crusade. For nearly 20 years, the Surgeon General's Report on Smoking stated that cigar smokers who smoked fewer than five cigars a day had the same mortality rate as nonsmokers. When that conclusion became politically unpalatable in the 1980s, the report's authors turned to other studies that surveyed European cigar smokers, citing the findings to bolster their claims that cigar smoking increased the risk of oral cancers. They failed to mention, of course, that the Europeans in the studies smoked 10 to 20 small, dry, cigarette-style cigars a day, and that they usually inhaled."

As a counterpoint, here are these excerpts from this (I think it's politically correct, but check, OK?) piece from Knight-Tribune News Service, around March of '97: "What an evil trend it is. Young, healthy people who have not succumbed to cigarettes are picking up cigars in increasing numbers. It's distressing," said Thierry Jahan, an oncologist... "The practice is an act of rebellion for some, a legal means of thumbing one's nose at the status quo..." [I pause here to remove the band from my Havana Partagas - which is down to an inch or so - and thumb my nose]..."Other than the psychological enjoyment there is no (health) benefit that is derived," said Mount Zion's Jahan [didn't someone say they were loaded with vitamin C?]..."How many of the people that are doing this as a recreational activity will unwittingly become addicted and turn to cigarettes, or start inhaling heavily their cigars?" (the American Cancer Society's Mr. Beerline) asked, "I think that it is a clear and present danger."

There, we have balance. Be sure to pick up a pack of Lucky's with your next corona and get ready to sue the Hondurans for providing such a gateway drug, without so much as a warning label (except, of course, in California) on the bundle.

Safest Form Of Tobacco Use

Quantifying a thing like this is nearly impossible, but I think it is fair to say that while smoking cigars almost certainly poses some risk to your health, it is probably the safest of the tobacco vices - pipe smokers mostly all inhale to some degree and get great jets of tar shot into their mouth, to boot; chewers tend to concentrate the wad of healthful material on only one area "between lip and gum," and cigarette smokers, well, they just pull all that garbage straight into their lungs, where the body has the devil's own time removing it. Especially, cigars are, without question, much better for you than cigarettes. Again, not good for you, but perhaps not so bad as many a newspaper would portray.

As this is written, a new "study" is all over the press, which concludes that cigar smoking is just as injurious as cigarettes. Specific data supporting this conclusion, at least in the popular press, is remarkably absent. We'll just have to wait and see how things develop, but know that smoking in any form is detested by some political forces, and that press-spinning and opinion-shaping ain't science.

Health & Smoking Safety

Safety Tips

Which brings us to the safety tip section. As we have mentioned, all risk is relative and the whole point of it (at least from the enlightened hedonist's perspective) is to maximize the pleasure while paring down the risk to our own precious arses.

The first tip is to never, ever, ever inhale! I know that this should go without saying, but if you have a physiology particularly well complemented by nicotine you may find the smoke creeping back farther and farther into your throat, perhaps emerging, after awhile, from your nose, or brushing the tops of your bronchial tubes. Even worse, pulled deeper into the lungs. This you must avoid, if inclined! Keep the smoke in your mouth only, where the saliva and beverage can wash its residue away. This will be particularly difficult for ex-cigarette smokers, especially those who are trying, without interruption, to substitute cigars for their cigarettes.

The technique can work, by the way, and improve your health and extend your lifespan dramatically. But you must never inhale. To do so is much worse than to smoke cigarettes, for cigar smoke is far thicker, and far more tar and nicotine laden, even if, as one author would have it, it is more "organic" and has a "more natural pH." Elephant cookies. It is much more harmful than cigarette smoke, if inhaled. Cigar smoke is thick, bearing grease compared to the light oil of cigarette smoke. As G.G. Liddy once said (or nearly so), "give me the nicotine from a few cigars, and I can have a man dead in a few hours." Although he was referring to extracting and concentrating the nicotine and using it as an oral poison, with food or drink, it is clear that there is an awful lot of the stuff in the things. If the smoke is taken in the mouth only, hardly any is absorbed into the body: blood nicotine levels are significantly lower than for cigarette smokers. Just don't inhale.

Remember these words that a man in a gun shop told me once when I was young: "you inhale that stuff and you'll be dead before your birthday, son." The folk wisdom is sometimes the best, after all.

The bottom line is that while cigar smoke has a lot more stuff in it (which is what gives it its flavor), limiting its exposure to the mouth only delivers a lot less to your system. As a lady, who had lost her cigarettes, once said as she sat in my lap, smoking a cigar, "it just doesn't give me that nicotine rush." Had she inhaled, she would have rushed to the powder room.

Know also that what cigar smoke - from quality, handmade cigars, not the kind that come wrapped in cellophane boxes - does have in it is all natural, for whatever that is worth. None of the chemicals - used to "enhance flavor" or "sustain addiction," depending on whose side of the judge's bench you sit - added to cigarette tobacco will be found here.

This brings up an interesting aside. Please don't kid yourself that using any form of tobacco is anything more than a nicotine delivery system, cause it ain't. No more than will the person whose biochemistry cares nothing for alcohol enjoy the exploration of fine wine or scotch, will the genetically-nicotine-abhorrent enjoy cigars.

Don't blame me for this truth, I did not deal the hand of your DNA. Some like some things, some don't, and that's the way it is. Those whose basic makeup favor nicotine will enjoy cigars and those whose don't will never understand how anyone could possibly take pleasure from it.

So if they ask, with disdain, why you smoke, reply that you simply can't help liking it. Sure seems to work for the gay population. And if you use this analogy, by the way, you are sure to put your politically-correct critics in one dizzy of a quandary.

It is interesting (actually, fascinating) to note that of some quite ancient Chinese mummies exhumed in the mid-'90's, about 30% carried evidence of nicotine use! The fascinating part is, how did the ancient Chinese get their hands on a plant which is widely believed to be Central and North American in origin? Could this be proof of an early Native American mafia, dealing, across great distance, with their cousins to the east? To this, the mid twentieth century Italian-Americans, with their tax "free" trucks of cigarettes from North Carolina, can hold no candle.

Sorry to digress, back to cigars.

Moderation

Two other important points to enhance your pleasure.

The first is that cigars, like so many things in life, are best enjoyed in moderation. Having a few tastes better than having too many. And, unless you follow our guidelines on cost-effective cigar shopping, will keep that second mortgage on the house at bay longer. Once-in-a-while is anticipated more, savored longer, remembered better, than all-the-time.

The other thing that I encourage you to do is to quit once in awhile. To prove to yourself that you can and to make that next cigar smell, to those who care, all the more sweet. Not only will this help to clear the palate, thus enhancing your future pleasure, but it will help your body to repair any minor damage you may have inflicted, free from the onslaught of all that lovely, swirling smoke.

CHAPTER THREE

The Basics Of The Beast

The Cigar Spectrum

Just the <u>big</u> cigars, please. While everything from the Winchester-style brown cigarettes to the hard, dried out Italian-type cheroots goes by the name cigar, our interest here is only in the larger, well constructed, humidified ("wet," in the trade) Cuban-style cigar. These are known in the cigar business as "big" cigars. It is this type of cigar that can be made with a blend of ingredients large and diverse enough to give fullness and nuance of flavor, and be built to produce ease of draw, firmness of feel, and plenty of eye appeal. The moistness of the tobacco - these cigars generally keep best in air with humidity of between 65-75% - helps to keep the smoke cool, reducing harshness and improving taste. Large, long pieces of tobacco are used as filler, slowing the burn rate and also helping to cool. This is referred to as "long filler," and in the best cigars runs the entire length of the smoke: each piece of filler is as long as the cigar is, and burns without interruption as the cigar is smoked. The binder - the tube that holds the filler leaves - and the wrapper are always tobacco, and chosen to polish the blend. These are most often made by hand entirely, or by hand using simple mechanical tools.

The "little," mass market cigars are made more like cigarettes, using finely chopped, chemically treated tobacco, wrapped in a paper tube like a cigarette. This is referred to as "short filler." These are found both dry (more popular in Europe than in the U.S.) and moist.

Between these and the really good cigars are mass market, "drug store" types that are made to look almost like the good ones, but are actually constructed more like cigarettes. Short filler, with a hole molded in the end to let the smoke through. Instead of tobacco binder leaf, these cigars use "homogenated" leaf - which is really a paper product made from chopped-and-chemically-processed tobacco, sold in sheets - to wrap the bunch. The box can legally say "100% tobacco" even though they use this "paper." Some of the better of this sort will wrap actual leaf over this binder, but don't be fooled. If you cut or bite the end off a cigar like this the way you do with a Cuban style cigar, the filler will run out, into your mouth and over your shirt, embarrassing you horribly. That can't happen with a long filler cigar, since the other end of the bit of filler in your mouth is burning on the far side of the cigar. Doesn't fall out easily.

Using the information you'll find later in this book, you'll be able to buy "real" cigars for about the same money as these drug store dandies, which you will enjoy much more, and prove far more effective in impressing your neighbors, than those papier-mâché stogies ever could.

Of course, there is more of a smooth progression of quality than just these three basic types, but that maps out the general categories. We will focus on the high end, Cuban style only, and explore them from the inexpensive, bundle types to the super premiums. Always we will consider value as well as quality. Finding the world's best cigar will provide little pleasure if you can afford to smoke only two per month.

Length of leaf is important enough to be brought up again, in a bit more detail. The best cigars use long filler, strips of tobacco running the entire length of the cigar. It is not all the same tobacco, but rather a blend which can combine as many as six different varieties - plus the binder and wrapper - in the larger diameter cigars which have room for them. Short filler cigars use finely chopped tobacco, as we have seen. But the other really important type is the so-called "sandwich" or medium filler cigar, where the basic construction is long filler, but is supplemented with pieces an inch or so long, which are generally the trimmings left over from the manufacture of more expensive cigars. Same tobacco, shorter pieces. While this can make for some irregularity of burn, these cigars are very good often enough - and very inexpensive all of the time, when accurately represented for what they are - that you should seriously consider them.

But first, a bit more detail on construction.

Cigar Construction

Every One Is Different

The first thing to remember is that we are dealing with a handmade product. At the upper end, every aspect of the operation is done completely by hand. Even at the lower end, where machine bunching - the formation, shaping, and insertion of the filler leaves into the binder - is used, the important stuff, like wrapping, binding, trimming, and capping is done by human only. The upside is that the cigar art, like most things human, can reach very lofty heights, indeed. The downside is that mistakes <u>will</u> happen and a certain percentage of even the most expensive, quality-controlled product will be unsmokable. When I was younger this used to bother me a great deal, to the extent where I would actually return - one end bit, one end black - those cigars whose construction did not meet my standards for draw and even burn. Some dealers actually accepted them back, at least for a time, though they seemed to welcome my business less and less. As I have mellowed with the hormonal dampening brought on by middle age, I now simply throw the bad ones away. I doubt that anyone would take them back in these days of cigar dealer kingdom, anyway.

The other thing to remember is that cigars are not automobiles, where the quality and availability of component materials does not vary much from time to time. Despite the cigar manufacturers' efforts - and they are good ones - to maintain consistency of appearance and taste through the years, the "same" cigar model actually varies quite a bit from month to month, even from batch to batch. Crops vary in quality, sometimes do not come in at all. Monsoons and droughts happen. A favored wrapper leaf may simply not be available in the quantities required, because of a poor crop, or because competitors have bought it up. Maintaining consistency in model and brand is like trying to paint the same picture over and over again, from an ever-changing palate of colors. Again, the manufacturers have done an admirable job, mostly by blending crops from year to year. This year's cigar has some of last year's crop in it and so will next year's cigar. No single-malt mentality here - the ingredients change too much.

How Cigars Are Rolled

Without getting into a lot of details that I am sure will bore you to no end, this is how a cigar is made. A handful of moist tobacco - the "bunch" is prepared in one of the ways described below and wrapped with binder leaf. This bunch is inserted into a cigar mold for the size and shape of the cigar being produced, and pressed a bit to give it the desired figure and consistency. It is removed from the mold and then covered in its expensive wrapper leaf, which both gives it lovely appearance and contributes a surprising amount to overall flavor. After that, the filler sticking out of each end is trimmed off with a knife. The end for your mouth is then "capped," where a bit of wrapper is shaped and glued (don't worry, no Elmer's here) on to complete the cigar. Less expensive cigars, to save on labor costs, are not capped but finished with a "curly-head," where the wrapper leaf on that end is not trimmed flush but simply twisted tight and left to dry. Neither type of head finish affects taste much. Of course, the most experienced and skillful rollers make the best and most expensive cigars, while those just starting out learn on the cheaper brands and shapes.   If you want to learn more than this about the actual rolling process, buy the other books, or mail me your questions. Wrap your questions in currency.

The Inevitable "Bad" Cigars

The most frequent cause of a bad unit is "plugging," where the cigar will not draw easily, and feels as if it is too tightly rolled.   And sometimes they <u>are</u> too tight.   But the draw problem most often has to do with a bit of filler leaf being folded back so that it blocks the passages in the cigar through which the smoke should pass.   Remember, with long filler, that the smoke must find its way through channels - it can not pass through the side of a leaf.   If the side of a leaf is in the way, the cigar is plugged.

The Cigar's Guts: Pick Them With Care

These channels are made through three basic techniques. The first, best, and by far most rarely found is called "entubar," for tubes.   Cigars made this way are always expensive (though because a cigar is expensive does not mean it is made this way) because of the time in workmanship required.   Basically, each filler leaf is rolled into a tube as long as the cigar is to be, a bunch of tubes are bunched, bound in binder leaf, wrapped and finished. The cigar burns evenly and draws easily, as smoke passes effortlessly through the tubes.

At the other end of the scale is the "book" technique, where the bunch is simply folded over, like a newspaper, and shoved into the mold, there to be cranked tight.   This is the worst type of bunch, often giving very tight draw and most uneven burn - the side of the cigar near the apex of the fold (or the "spine" of the book), having more tobacco packed more tightly together, burns much more slowly that the other side.   The result is often enough a thorough mess that you should avoid this type completely.

Although this is often the reason that a cigar may not burn evenly, there are two other possible causes. The slower burning tobacco - the ligero (explained in a moment; be patient, tobacco-leaf-hopper) - may be on one side of the cigar instead of in the middle, where it belongs. Or a wad of filler - a dense point - may be pushed to one side, with a too-loose section opposite. Whatever the reason, this type of burn makes for a very unhappy period of smoking. It will usually correct itself, if you buck up and keep smoking, but I now through 'em away if this happens, since the taste during the time of the uneven burn can be horrible.

By the way, you don't have to dissect a cigar to find out how it is made, though that way tells the most. But just looking at the business end of the unlit cigar tells a lot. You can see the tubes, the book, or the folds of the next technique.

And note that the book may be a spiral, like taking a complete newspaper, and rolling it into a cylinder. Don't look much like a book, but booked nonetheless. When you look, get a feel for how tight the folds are jammed together. Too tight, and that's how the beast will smoke. Sleepily and niggardly, fighting you for every puff of smoke. Too loose, and you will have a roaring dragon in your hand, plumeing smoke and spouting bile. You want a baby bear sort of fold density. Just right. When so, the cigar will feel, and spring back, just like a roll of expensive toilet paper. Or something like that. Or, to analogize slightly bluer, "awfully pneumatic," as Huxley had it in <u>Brave New World</u>. Though, of course, he was referring to something ultimately much moister than any cigar.

The best compromise technique (sorry I don't know the Spanish word for it) works like this: several bits of filler are grabbed, and folded, back and forth, like a roadmap, or like corrugated cardboard. I call it the accordion method. Folded less than perfectly and very quickly, but still in such a way that the cigar burns evenly and draws smoothly. This style carries a higher probability of getting a plugged cigar, but when done without error - which is often enough for me - the draw is as easy as for entuber. Nearly all cigars in the "best buy" universe are made in this way. In fact, the entuber technique is so labor intensive that it is now very rarely encountered, no matter what you pay.

Information on construction method is rarely given in the marketing material or packaging; you have to look for yourself.

What "Hand Made" Really Means

Made by hand may not be, at least not completely. Often a cigar is offered as hand made, when in reality the cigar is machine bunched, perhaps machine rolled, and only hand finished. The descriptions we find on the boxes, and in the ads, are of only limited use, not only because they are often in Spanish, but because of the laxity with which they are applied. "Hencho a mano," made by hand, can be used in most producer countries to describe cigars which have even just a small amount of hand work, such as final finish. "Totmente a mano," completely by hand, is self explanatory, but rarely seen. And what about labels in English? J.R. Ultimates, undoubtedly one of the very best non-Cuban premium cigar lines, state simply that they are "Made by Hand," on their beautifully made mahogany box. A Nicaraguan bundle says the same thing on its slip of a white paper label glued haphazardly to the cellophane, but about it I have less confidence, though the cigars are generally good and an excellent buy. Which brings us to the point: quality of construction and material is far more important than the extent of hand workmanship. While it is true that in the very best, most expensive cigars, highly skilled craftsmen turn out consistent, excellent quality product, this is nearly always not true for lesser brands, even those very well regarded, even if they are "totmente a mano." For instance, I am at the moment smoking a Cuban Partagas Aristocrat, purchased in Rome. It is an excellent cigar, but more because of the Cuban tobacco than because it is completely hand made: I've had more than a few partially plugged cigars in this box. Some Cuban Belinda Belvederes, bought in the Bahamas, gave more consistent quality, even though they appear to be "totalmente a machino," although it does not of course say this on the box. So remember: unless you can both afford and believe it is wise to buy only the best, very expensive cigars (remembering that very expensive on its own means very little), it is better to focus on quality of construction, leaf, and length of filler, than on extenta a mano.

Same Brand, Different Country: Yes, We Have No Habanas

I emphasis the Cuban above, to make an important point. There now exist I the world at least two <u>totally</u> distinct varieties of each established great brand. Two Hoyo de Monterry, two Partagas, two H. Upman, two Punch, and so on. One made in Cuba, one not. And often nearly indistinguishable in packaging and banding, but for the Habana to be found only on the one. Of course, U.S. smokers, who both stay in the U.S. and do not haunt the black market, will see only one, at least for a little while longer. And for those who haunt, beware the counterfeit, which makes up the bulk of the U.S. "Cuban" supply, at least on the street, and from at least one otherwise respectable Cuban pharmaceutical salesman that I know in Jacksonville. I even bought him lunch, for goodness sake. More on spotting the bogus goods later, for those who believe in the words of Nino, the great Roman tour guide, who says: "here, many things are forbidden... but we do them anyway...." (Nino also says, on the Vatican Swiss Guards, that this is because "Italians are not good for guarding...Italians are good...for other things." On showing a picture of his young daughter, he says, "Look...what Nino...make." And on the lack of crowds when he shows us the Sistine Chapel in the afternoon, when it had been thronged in the morning, he croons, "This is not a miracle...this...is Neeeeno.").

This dichotomy of brands exists, of course, as a direct result of the Cuban communist revolution, and the subsequent U.S embargo. It is interesting to note that Kennedy, a devoted cigar smoker, was careful to lay in a vast supply of his beloved coronas before trade was choked off. Almost as interesting that Marv Shanken, editor of <u>Cigar Aficionado</u>, paid upwards of half a million dollars for Kennedy's humidor when it finally appeared in Jackie O's estate auction in 1996.

With the advent of the Castro regime, many of Cuba's capitalistic cigar makers fled the homeland, to found new empires <u>with the same brand names</u>, mostly in the Dominican Republic and in Honduras. Cuba - whose other major export is sugar, which needs no brand - "nationalized" and kept the popular and profitable brand names, the better to finance the poverty of the Cuban people. And please, no jokes about selling Fidel the rope by which he may hang us. The fellow can't afford string, for gosh sakes. What is most interesting is what will become of this brand situation, when relations with the jewel of the Caribbean are finally normalized. And for the record, they are abnormal only with the U.S. My hunch is that they will continue to compete as separate entities, just like they do now, everywhere but in the land of the free. In any event, know that there are two and that just because the Dominican Partagas (long widely regarded as the best constructed cigar in the non-Cuban world) is made entubar, the Cubans ain't necessarily. In fact, at this very moment, my humidor holds several boxes of Partagas Habanos (in my opinion the best buy in Cuban cigars these days, at about a quarter the cost of Fidel's Cohibas, which are very good, but not four-times-the-cost-of-Partagas good), some marked totally by hand, some marked merely made in Cuba, which, of course, means machine made.

A Note On Brands

You'll notice that for the most part, we aren't saying an awful lot about the merits of particular brands. Oh, it will crop up here and there, as in the last section, to make particular points, and there will be a chapter on my favorites, later on. But we will not get goofy about it, it the sense that this book is "The Ultimate Guide To The World's Best Cigar Brands," or anything like that. The reason is that such a book, even if an author could collect all the existing information is this so mercurial of markets, would be completely out of date before it was finished. Things change far too rapidly. The quality and taste of existing brands varies greatly form month to month, and new brands spring up as fast as others disappear. A cigar factory is not like a Rolex factory which produces only Rolexes. Each factory may produce many brands and in many cases the same cigars go out under different brands. Heck, more often than not, the brand is decided <u>after</u> the cigars are made and sorted. The same cigar may be banged out and shipped with minimum aging for a medium grade brand and aged much longer to become a super premium. Cigars intended to be one brand, but which exhibit manufacturing flaws may be shipped as another brand - and these often represent very good buys. And so on. The market is ever shifting, full of quicksand. So we will instead try to give you a good, durable, general guide, instead of a definitive and shortly-useless catalog.

If you are looking for such a definitive list, the very best source I know of is <u>Cigar Aficionado</u> (we'll refer to it as C.A. from now on; about $20 for 6 issues per year; PO Box 51091/ Boulder, CO 80323-1091; 800-992-2442), a wonderful magazine which in each issue publishes an extensive "blind tasting" of a large number of cigars, from different makers and countries, which fit a given size/shape category. The reviews are good, even if they do wax a bit "wine-world" verbose: "...an overtone of sweet cocoa bean and hints of nutmeg and cinnamon. A sweet cedar, coffee bean finish." Of course, describing a taste is never easy. This gives us fairly comprehensive reviews of many shapes from this source each year and the magazine has collected (and probably will again) several years worth of reviews into a book, <u>Cigar Aficionado Buying Guide to Premium Cigars</u>. Just remember, when using such a source, how quickly things can change in the world of cigars. The cigars that you are able to buy by the time you read the reviews are likely to be far different than those used in the tests. SMOKE magazine also offers such reviews and is another great magazine, though slightly-less-taken with its own importance than is C.A. Ordering info for SMOKE appears later in the "paper resources" chapter.

The Ideal Cigar Draw

Some guys (and gals!) like 'em tight. Some like 'em loose. As Billy Joel sang, "A bottle of red, a bottle of white, it all depends upon your appetite." For the most part. But within a rather limited range, some things are absolute. The cigar should burn evenly and slowly. But not too slowly, as when a "knot" of too-tightly packed filler somewhere in the tube almost prevents it from burning at all. Draw should be nearly effortless, but with a slight bit of "tug" required: a draw which is too easy means the cigar is packed too loosely, and will burn fast, harsh, hot, and probably unevenly. This will be evident to you without a detailed description from me. A draw which is too hard - needing more then just a gentle suction - is, in my opinion, a thing from Hell itself. I have heard tell that some guys like it that way - can't imagine why - but I find that having to work at pulling smoke from the cigar kills almost all the pleasure for me. Smoke around and form your own opinions. Of course, a good draw and even, slow burn is completely the result of sound construction: proper tension and distribution of filler, and arrangement of filler - entuber or "accordion" - so that it does not impede the passage of smoke.

And, by the way, a cigar which is tough to draw before you light it, is sure to tighten up - like your first real date when things got hot- after you light it. The reason, I think, is that the water in the smoke - water being a principal byproduct of combustion - swells the leaf further back in the cigar, exacerbating the plug. We will give you a few tips on surgery later in the repair section, but the prognosis is not good. If you have any hope of returning a plugged cigar, your chances are probably better if you do not actually light it.

A good way to check for draw - and an indication of over-all quality - is to <u>feel</u> the cigar and squeeze it just a bit. A well made cigar with the correct amount of filler will be firm but resilient, kinda springy, like a tire with 20 psi or so of pressure. An underfilled - which will usually be only in spots, so be careful - cigar will stay dented when squeezed even gently. And you must be gentle. An overfilled smoke will feel rock hard and be obviously packed too tight when you examine construction from the lightable end. It will draw tighter than Scrooge, burn too slow, and go out often even if you resign yourself to smoking it. Under-filling makes for a hot, harsh, fast burn. Springy filling makes for just right.

Categories of Quality: Super Premium to the Bundle In The Bag

We're about to enter a world of twilight, a world where shapes and realities shift, where the drums of the market-ing tribes pulse loudly, and where spirits dance to the beat of pleasures they do not taste.

We will brush broad strokes and try to point out the sign-posts that have meaning. Remember, in the modern world of the super-popular cigar, hype nearly rules, and you must learn to read the tea leaves and chicken bones for yourself. We will give you the guidebook, but you must roll the bones for yourself.

Let's make one thing clear: in the world of cigars, few things are perfectly clear! My definitions of the categories below, for instance, are very subjective, and merely my opin-ions of how things seem to work. The definitions vary a bit from smoker to smoker and from source to source. Even the maker's traditions are often at odds: the word for a cigar shape and size, like Churchill, Centro, or Sabrosas, can de-scribe a completely different cigar, depending on who makes it, and what they decide to slap on the box. Even the word clear is unclear! A "clear" Havana, you see, is not transpar-ent, but tells us that a smoke is made entirely from Cuban tobacco, though some would insist that it also be made in

Cuba to be <u>really</u> clear. Fear not. We will guide you with intelligence, fine research, and common sense, so that you will be invested with the real meanings of the words. I think.

The Super-Premium

First, a sniff into the rarefied, cedar-scented airs of the super premium. These cigars are marketed as the creme de la creme, the very top of a given manufacturer's line. Examples would be the Punch Gran Cru series, the Hoyo de Monterry Excaliburs (these two both made in Honduras by the same house, Villizon, based in New Jersey), the Dominican Partagas' 1845 Limited Reserves, and the (also Dominican) Arturo Fuente Opus X's. We must also include the J.R. Ultimate series, also made in Honduras by Villizon for the J.R. Tobacco discount house, arguably the largest cigar retailer in the world. These last, by the way, are probably the cheapest super premiums on the market, and represent excellent value, if you like them.

Super premium, as defined here, means cigars made - and marketed - to be of superlative quality. Often these are the very highest quality of a given producer's output, with quality dropping as we move "down the line." Sometimes a manufacturer will make (or contract a factory to make) only cigars like these. Prices vary widely. The J.R. Ultimates mentioned above can be had, depending on size, for a few dollars apiece. The most expensive of the non-Cuban world have been offered at prices approaching $25. And I have seen single Cohibas offered in Nassau at over $50 U.S. per cigar. If you buy one, pray it is not plugged! But it is wrong to consider only the most expensive for this category, since some truly superb smokes can be had for very reasonable prices.

These cigars are most often very plushly packaged and slickly advertised. But remember to examine the book, not just glance at the cover. While the super premiums of the more established, respected makers <u>usually</u> offer consistently superior quality, one must beware the onslaught of apparently new super premiums, which look great in ad and box, but may not have much of a tradition of excellence. A casual glance into the current C.A. reveals many lovely, one- and two-page ads for brands I have never heard of and I have been smoking good cigars for about 25 years. These ads are hugely expensive - and reflected in pricing, to be sure - but tell us nothing of the actual quality.

Use what you are learning in this book, instead. Some of these upstarts may be very good, but buy one, if enchanted, examine and taste it, before falling in love. And if the allure of the super premiums appeals to you, at least start with those from the long standing, fine houses, like Fuente, Partagas, Punch, H. Upman, Don Diego, Don Thomas, Hoya de Monterry, Joya de Nicaragua, Macanudo, Montecruz, Royal Jamaica, Te-Amo, and Zino. There, I have done it! Given you a list of some of the major, long standing lights in the non-Cuban sky. And don't worry if your favorites (or your products, dear manufacturer) don't appear above; we'll get into far more detail on the brands with staying power later in the book. But these are the brands that have been familiar to me (even if some don't suit my particular tastes) for a very long time, from back in the days when everyone knew that all cigar smokers were scum. Now, of course, the non-smokers only <u>suspect</u> this.

All in all, while the super premiums are often at the pinnacle of the cigar maker's art, lovely to behold and taste, I think that they are rarely worth the price. Even if you are only a very occasional smoker, I think that you would do far better to smoke cigars that are nearly as good, but cost far less.

A subset of the super premium would be the vintage cigar, usually applied to cigars made entirely from tobacco of a particularly good year. Sometimes they are just old cigars that just never came to be smoked. And yes, the tobacco is aged, both before and after it is turned into cigars. The more expensive the cigar, theoretically, the more time and attention give to aging. And, for what it is worth, you will from time to time get cigars - in nearly every category - that smoke "green"...harsh, a bit hot, obviously not ready. When this happens, be patient, and give them some time in your humidor. You will be surprised at the result after even a few months. But I do not believe that aging beyond a few years at the outside helps flavor and probably detracts from it.

Here is an example, not of super premiums but of expensive cigars in general, to prove the price-does-not-equal-quality relationship. In the same CA issue's tasting of Robustos, the second most highly rated non-Cuban cigar is the El Rico Habana Habano Club (don't let the Habano on the band fool you - these babies come from Hispanola), ranking a very high score of 90, and a retail price of $3.25. Much farther down the list is the also-Dominican Paul Garmirian Robusto, with a score of 81 and a price of $8.30! Not that next month's Garmirians may not be sublime, but the price spread is huge. And, by the way, the 83-scored Las Cabrillas Cortez, from Honduras, can be had for $1.80. The point again being that there is a loose relationship, at best, between quality and price. So don't you be had.

That advice holds for the premiums below, as well. These cigars are best reserved for special occasions, or where you want a "power cigar" to make an impression, either by smoking or gifting it. But, forgive me, the impression it makes upon me is one of waste and perhaps, ignorance.

Premium Cigars

These are those near, but not quite at, the top of a given maker's line.

Examples might be the A. Fuente Gran Reserva line, and nearly everything in the non-Cuban Partagas line except the 1845 Limited Reserves series. Also the Fuente Hemingway line. The larger and more expensive sizes from Punch and Hoya de Monterry, Gran Cru and Excalibur, of course, excluded. You get the picture. When these cigars can be found at reasonable prices, they are very good value. But while the posted wholesale prices on these have not gone up all that much (I know this because I have a wholesale account with Villazon), supply is very short and most retailers have jacked their prices unmercifully. And we can hardly blame them, since they have a very hard time getting replacement product when the cigars fly off their shelves.

Again, many suspect that the "shortage" of the old time smokes - in this day when more cigars are being made than ever before in history - is due more to the transformation of the old line stuff into nouveau super premiums which can be sold at enormous profit, than to any real lack of supply.

But whatever, the premiums, and those in the category to follow, are good, when you can get them fairly. But still far from the best buys, since they cost more and still suffer from the ills of hand-making that plague most output. For instance, I was recently fortunate to get two boxes of one of my very favorite brands, in a premium size. Nearly every cigar in the first box was wonderful. But 75% of the second box was bad, rolled too tight (too much filler in the bunch for the mold size) and mostly plugged, to boot. At about $60 for the 25 in the box, that brought the average cost of the six good cigars to about $10. And no, I did not sleep with them, but I was tempted. This kind of roulette is a lot easier to take when the cigars don't cost so much to begin with.

Brand Cigars

These are the bread and butter, the Chevrolets, of most of the established manufactures. They can be the middle and lower ends of a particular manufacturer's line, or a separate brand name from the same maker, where he sells the same (or similar) cigars under another marque at a lower price point. An example would be the Bances brand, made by Villizon (again, maker of Punch and Hoyo de Monterry) but sold for less than the flagship brands.

One thing to bear in mind as you move down a given line, though it should not concern you too much. There is clearly less hand work as we go down the line, with the bottom products possibly being nearly completely machine made. This should not matter so long as construction is sound, since the similar quality of leaf and blend is usually used in them. But be aware. Villizon's Punch London Club, for instance, is made by machine in Tampa of Honduran long filler. And it is a decent cigar, at a decent price. Finding these cigars on the tobacconist's humidor shelves is usually pretty easy: they're the cheaper ones in a given brand name. Fuente, for instance, has one of the most extensive lines in the business, from super premiums in the $10+ range, to those offered at less than a buck. So they are easy to find, provided the retailer can still manage to stock a decent selection. If he suffers from the shortage, about the only thing to do is to look for brands you recognize and models that seem to be fairly priced. Again, try only one or so from each box that appeals to you. If you find something you like and the price is right, buy every box on the shelves, if the dealer will let you. And, by the way, you used to be able to get a discount (off the single price times the number in the box) if you bought the whole box. No more. In fact, they may not sell you the whole box of a recognizable name, just to keep something on the shelves. Gee whiz, I know one dealer who sells the empty boxes and insisted on her price even though I'd bought over $100 worth of "singles" from her, and had nothing to put them in! Haven't been back there, in awhile.

One last word on brand cigars, to strike another note of caution. I recently got a rather expensive bundle banded by a very famous and respected maker. The cigars were in every way the same quality, at first glance, as the maker's high end product, except for the packaging, and they cost a lot. I'm now halfway through and have not yet had one that was good. In disgust, I recently dissected the last one I lit up, after it yet again started with a very uneven burn and a hot, harsh taste. The cigar was a "sandwich," despite the bundle being marked "long filler," and what long filler was inside was booked, explaining the uneven burn. The pieces of short filler were packed in seemingly at random, giving alternating loose and tight spots along the length. Caveat smoker. Shop carefully and sample until you find something you like, before you load up.

Bundle Cigars

Ah... Now we are getting to the territory that appeals to the value- investing, bottom-fishing kind of guy that I am.

First a bit of history on the development of the bundle, and then quickly to the current state of the art.

By the way, a bundle is simply bunch of cigars - usually 20 or 25, just like a box - which are unceremoniously gathered together, wrapped in cellophane, and sold that way, with or without bands. The packaging is nearly expense-less. Sometimes the wrapped bundle has a paper label glued to it.

Bundle cigars began as a way to dispose of "seconds," those cigars, because of wrapper blemish or other production flaw, which did not meet the standards of the brand. The packaging was a joke, but they were sold at deep discounts, and often smoked as well as the "perfect" ones in the branded box. Clearly these were great deals and some still can be found, but only through a knowledgeable tobacconist who hunts them down and actually knows what he has when he gets it. Obviously, the makers are not real keen on seeing these seconds sold as "As good as Joyo de Grande Joyo. In fact, they are Joyos!, at 1/3 the cost!" At least in the old days, this just might tend to hamper demand for the "real" Joyos just a bit. Nowadays, I suspect that fewer and fewer seconds are being distributed this way, since it is just to easy to concoct another Super Premium brand, pump 'em out at inflated prices, and risk no adverse reflection on the primary brand. Or simply sell them to an entrepreneur with his own new brand, which amounts to the same thing in the mouth of the cigar smoker.

The bundle trick proved to be a successful way to move cigars, and is now used as a "normal" packaging technique. Which is to say that cigars are expressly made to become bundle cigars. I think that there are several reasons for this. For one thing, the package costs almost nothing, and if the maker can get almost as much for each cigar, he makes more. For another, bundle cigars have come to be regarded by the buying public as "all right," not necessarily indicative of an inferior grade. So much so that many legitimate brands, or models in brand lines, are sold this way and no other. The modern key to remember with bundles is this: like price, the package says nothing about the quality of the cigar. They may be wonderful, they may be stable-sweepings trash. So look, taste, and tell. But this area represents the greatest opportunity for deep discount purchase of quality product than any other in the cigar universe.

I emphasis that quality can vary widely. I've been lately smoking a brand called Mocha, from Honduras, a good size bought in bundles of 20 for $12.95 from J.R. Tobacco. The cigars are excellent and, though I'd never heard of the brand before, I was surprised to find it by Bati in his The Cigar Companion (Running Press, 1995), which for the most part is a "brand catalog" book. Bati says the cigars are mild and are sold boxed, though they are neither, at least right now. They are as fine a deal as I have had. At the other end, I've paid more for cigars made in the same city in Honduras, which came 50 to the brown-bag bundle, and were just horrible. Poor draw, hot burn, uneven burn up the side. Booked. I don't think there was a good smoke in the 50. So again, beware, and check it out. Like price, let not the package alone be your guide. But watch out for brown bags.

These days, bundle cigars are available from nearly every source that deals in cigars at all. Every U.S. tobacconist I've visited sports more than a few. Most of the catalogs that pepper my mailbox have 'em. Even the major drugstore chains in my area have their own bundle brands, though quality, at least for Hondurans (my favorite non-Cuban country) varies, and prices are a bit high for the quality offered. The few drugstore Dominicans I've sampled have been O.K., if a bit bland (but most Dominicans taste that way to me), but much more expensive. And the bundles in most drugstores hold only eight or ten cigars.

Selecting good bundle cigars can be tough, since they can come in such bewildering variety, and may be here today, gone tomorrow as the output that is today's bundle is distributed in another manner tomorrow, or disappears altogether as the factory and materials are contracted for another cigarian purpose. So sample what you find and stock up on what you like - we'll show you how to store en-mass later on. When buying at a retail store, you can often find bundles broken, the cigars binned, and available as singles, so you can try one or two before jumping in. With the mail order discounters, you must buy a whole bundle. Not as bad as it sounds, though, since the package can often be had for less than the cost of two super premiums, and if you don't like them, you can always save them to give to friends who are very happy to have a cigar, even if they are not sure which end to light. Trust me, they'll be just as happy (perhaps just as green) with these, as they would be with one of your most cherished stash.

Initial supplies for a some bundle types are often very large - thousands and thousands - but once gone, they may not be back for awhile, if at all. And will surely be different, even if you find them again. I was rather painfully reminded of this just today, as I tried to order more of the above mentioned Mocha's from J.R., who currently, in the interest of rationing, limits buys to four bundles/boxes of a given variety each day. I'd been buying four bundles each day that I had time and remembered. We have been out of town for the last ten days or so and, at last word, they had nearly 100,000 bundles in stock. Today, they tell me they have none! And I must be on the hunt again. So stock up when you have the chance.

The one exception would be the old-line brand bundles - like Don Mateo and Riata - which are branded (and banded) products designed for long term market recognition, which simply happen to have forgone the expense of box packaging, though you usually get a nice bright label on the bundle. With these, you can expect the same efforts on the part of the makers to maintain consistency of flavor and quality from year to year and pretty much perennial availability, at least so far. They should cost less because of the package, but otherwise be evaluated by you pretty much as any other branded product.

Also, sometimes branded bundles appear because of a "matching" screw up between cigar and box production on the part of a manufacturer: they wind up with more cigars than they have boxes for. Instead of selling the output otherwise - like under another of the house's brands, or to a broker who will "create" his own, perhaps short lived brand with them - they may simply be wrapped in pretty paper and sold as bundles.

Finally, you may see some cigars packed as bundles simply because the maker feels like it. I remember getting some La Gloria Cubana (the U.S. made sort) - a super premium on anyone's scale - a few years back at a mall near Miami. The cigars came beautifully bundle packed - more like a Christmas present, with lovely printed paper - but still cost me a bundle!

Enough of the basics! Time to move on to the finer points of cigar anatomy, like size and shape, color, country, taste characteristics, that sort of thing. Actually the points are not that much finer, but its time for a chapter break, and this excuse provides a good segueway. Smoke on!

CHAPTER FOUR

A Cigar's Finer Points...
The Beauty Of The Beast

Cigar Anatomy

There are three basic components of any "big" cigar and, of course, they must all be of tobacco, in fact, are very specialized sorts of tobacco. They are the binder, the blend or filler, and the wrapper. They are more or less of increasing importance and we will take them that way.

Binder

This is the stuff that holds the whole shebang together and is a specialized leaf engineered as much for strength as flavor. Think of it as the "body" of the cigar, with the wrapper as the "paint." As you recall from our prior discussion, the filler leaves are prepared - rolled or more often, carefully folded - rolled in the binder and squeezed, gently, in the mold to give the new cigar its shape, before being covered in the wrapper leaf, trimmed, and finished. While the binder is very important, this is about all you need to know about it. Just make sure it's not that curious brown paper they make down in Tampa!

Blend

Let's move on to the cigar's blend. Not to show you how to make one, but to give an idea of what makes a cigar's flavor tick.

The simple thing about filler leaf blend is that there are three basic varieties: **ligero**, from the top of the plant, richest in flavor, oiliest, darker in color, and slowest burning; **seco** leaves, from the middle of the plant, lighter in appearance and taste, and **volado**, nearly flavorless, but good-burning. For a one-crop cigar, these would be mixed in different proportions, depending on how robust and flavorful a cigar one wished to produce. When bunching, the stronger leaves usually are positioned nearer the middle of the cigar. Note that since a good hunk of long leaf - sometimes an entire leaf, stem and all - is used for each blend component, the number of ingredients possible is determined by the girth of the cigar, with the upper limit being 5 or 6 for the widest cigars. Thinner cigars might have only 2, or perhaps struggle with 3. Of course, "sandwich" cigars, which incorporate small pieces (still an inch or better, though), can include more types.

The complicated thing is that many plants, in fact, leaf from many countries, can be used in the modern cigar. This expands the cigar maker's palate to practical infinity, which explains the wide spectrum of tastes that different cigars can give. Still, consistency from year to year is a dicey thing, since last year's beloved leaf is a burnin' in the wind, and next year's is still a question mark. Which, again, is why they save some from each year, like master scotch blenders, to smooth out the variations. As an example, from the description of a Punch Chateau, from an old C.A.: Filler: Honduras, Nicaragua, Dominican Republic; Binder: Honduras; Wrapper: U.S.A. Connecticut Broadleaf. But it don't gotta be. From the same issue, the much more highly rated Padron reads: Nicaragua, Nicaragua, Nicaragua, Pepsi. Probably from the same fields. Just like the good old days.

Wrapper

This bit is really the soul of the cigar. Arguments rage in the cigar clubs as to just how much the wrapper contributes to overall flavor, but all agree it is significant. Almost as important, it is the wrapper, and only the wrapper (besides size, shape, and band, all of which pale by comparison once you really look) which creates your overall impression of just what the cigar is like. Silky and smooth, or rough and "toothy." Jade green, colorado "red," leather brown, or coffee black. Or coffee-and-creme tan. Richly veined, or surprisingly uniform. Lovely and perfect, or blotched but still tasty. And so on. Like a person's appearance, the wrapper gives us the first impression. And, as you will see, like people, the first impression is often hopelessly misleading, but lasting.

The wrapper is the most expensive leaf on the cigar and usually graded by appearance only. High grade wrapper leaf nearly glistens with oil, is uniform and unblemished, and nearly glows its color, whatever its color may be. It should also taste good. The best stuff is getting to be in pretty short supply and now wraps the premiums and better brand grades only.

By comparison, the wrappers on the Mochas we talked about before are just about downright ugly. Nondescript brown. No luster. More veins than is fashionable. And some visible blemishes, or "sunspots." Definitely second rate stuff, from an appearance (and hence a dollar value) standpoint. But they taste damn good. If it bothered me, I'd put a paper bag over it before I smoked it. But it doesn't. Flavor, like character in people, is the ultimate attribute. But this does give me occasion to comment once again on the tobacco "shortage." As we mentioned before, there is now more quality tobacco under cultivation than ever before in the history of the race. Truly record numbers of large cigars cranked out on an annual basis, and the demand keeps raising the bar, which the makers happily each year meet.

But good wrapper tobacco is a precious commodity. There is just not enough to go around, and this has been evident for at least several years now. True cameroon wrapper - not just with the name, but actually from the African country that gave the variety the name - is lovely, priceless, and delicious, but scarcely seen on today's market. So I think that what we have is a shortage of attractive cigars. In fact, I'd give long odds that in many cases the same cigar is sold as super premium, brand, and bundle, depending on the wrapper available in which the bunch is swathed. There are more good cigars than ever, but because of the wrapper bottleneck, they are mostly ugly cigars. Remember that often the ugly will taste as sweet, if only you will close your eyes.

Back to wrapper attributes. Remember that a big part of cigar flavor comes from the color. But not all of it. My humidor currently holds two boxes of a certain maker's super premiums, each a different size, but with the same gorgeous light brown wrappers. My favorite color. The corona size repeatedly smokes just wonderfully - deep, complex, strong. The churchills are just as repeatedly thin, weak, and boring. Same wrapper, different blend. Big difference in blend, given that the churchill is a 10-guage fire compared to the .410 of the corona. In desperation, I throw the churchill out (again) and torch up another of my beloved (though dwindling) Cuban Partagas. And am instantly in Heaven.

First we'll give you what you need to know about the four basic colors - though the middle two are often condensed into one for all practical purposes - before giving the words describing each nuance of shade (though brace yourself for the laughter if you try ordering a box that is "precisely colorado maduro" or "single claro only, please") that you can use to impress your friends at the cigar clubs. And note that the tastes I ascribe to especially the darker colors reflect my own opinions, formed over the decades, and with which most of today's cigar authors may not agree. Once again, beauty is in the mouth of the beholder, each sees a slightly different world, and you must, in the end, taste for yourself.

Before I begin, know that I like my cigars strong, robust, and with a great depth of flavor. Perhaps this is because my palate is so dense that only the loudest notes strike through, though I have always preferred them this way, even in my youth.

Oh, the wrapper also serves the high function of sealing the cigar, preventing leaks and ensuring that you get smoke instead of air when you draw. Sometimes, less expensive cigars will be found with wrapper "patches," bits of leaf that have been applied to repair holes or tears in imperfect wrappers. When they are there, they are hardly noticeable, and in no way affect flavor or performance.

Colors

The four basic colors are green, light brown (tan, really), slightly darker, reddish-brown, and nearly black-brown. To me, the green tastes sweet, spicy, hinting of fresh leaves, and with a limited depth of flavor. The light brown is to me the strongest, with great depth and complexity of flavor. They really sing to me, though I have found them very hard to find in this color in recent years. The reddish brown I find as flavorful as the light brown, with greater depth of flavor. The almost black I find surprisingly mild, very shallow and bland, almost dead.

By the bye, the color of the leaf is determined by two things: the part of the plant it came from (top, middle, or bottom), and the degree of fermentation to which it is subjected. The fermentation process consists of throwing a pile of leaves into a corner and letting them stew in their own juices, with biological processes and the tropical heat thrown in, until they are ready to be aged in a more dignified manner on their way to the cutting and rolling rooms. All right, the process is a bit more sophisticated than that, but you get the idea. The darker the leaf to begin with, and the longer the fermentation, the darker the end product.

The proper names (though the guys in the business still call double claro "green") are as follows:

- **Claro Claro** or **Candela**: the green above, in the past referred to as A.M.S. (for American Market Selection, because that's the way the old boys here used to like 'em; think of McArthur's - or my Dad's- cigars).
- **Claro**: a very light brown, with perhaps a bit of yellow, seldom seen but very good.
- **Colorado Claro**: light brown, tan.
- **Colorado**: Medium brown, often with hints of red. Probably the most common color today, though they do seem to be getting darker.
- **Natural or E.M.S.**: Encompasses the range of light and medium browns from claro to colordo. Used interchangeably, though the dealers will argue with you, but just look at the colors, and what the boxes say, for yourself. E.M.S. for English Market Selection, because the British have always had good sense.
- **Colorado Maduro**: Dark brown, losing flavor.
- **Maduro**: Very dark brown, and I think, bland. I know that many say that some maduros (generally used to denote any dark brown cigar, which is how you should use it) are rich and flavorful, but I have never met one. And I do, occasionally, look. I have a black, stockbroker friend, from the Islands, whose last name is Maduro, who is not amused when I remind him that, in my world, his name means "dark wrapper." He says, because of the trees on my lot, that I live in a "jungle house," just to get even with me, I think.
- **Oscuro**: So dark as to be black. A lovely, very inviting color, which seems to promise a great richness of flavor, but which has always disappointed me.

There you have the official list, to do with as you please. But I think that "green, light brown, reddish brown, and black brown" will serve you better, especially if you remember that "natural" and "E.M.S." mean the middle two and will probably give the most pleasure. But try the others. Green, especially, can make for a very interesting change of pace. And you may find that maduro really comes alive when you light it.

Let's look at some regions especially noted for quality wrapper leaf. The ole U.S. of A. - and in New England, for gosh sakes - produces some of the finest wrapper leaf known on a relatively tiny patch of soil in Connecticut. Connecticut Shade is so rare, and so revered, that according to one source its presence can add between $0.50 and $1.00 to the retail price of a cigar. Cameroon, a nation about halfway down Africa on the west coast, also produces world-class wrapper which nowadays seems always in short supply. Ecuador has been lately producing increasing quantities of excellent stuff. And wrapper from Sumatra, an island in Indonesia, has long been renowned by some, though I am not much of a fan. All of the primary cigar making nations also grow their own wrapper to some extent, which is what you will see on the lower priced output, and increasingly on the more expensive stuff as well. Of the exotic types, Connecticut and Cameroon (true Cameroon, as opposed to Cameroon seed tobacco, grown in a basement in Texas) are considered the best and are the rarest and costliest. Of course, these names will only be useful if you somehow come to know what's around your cigar - say from a C.A. review - or become so adept as to be able to tell from sight and feel alone.

Shape And Why Size Matters

Let's get through shape first, because there really isn't that much variation. Yes, there are some special ones and we'll get to them in just one bit. But the vast majority are simply cylinders, with only two important dimensions: diameter and length. Length, for the most part, is only important as it relates to how long the cigar will smoke - how much time you want to spend smoking. Although the build-up of smoke residue, and it's effect on taste, is greater in a longer cigar as you near the end than in a shorter one, this is really a very minor issue. Do note that the longer cigar will smoke cooler, for awhile, since there is a greater distance between the fire and your mouth. The diameter, or ring gauge (or just ring), of a cigar is so important that we must wait a moment before talking about it.

So the basic shape of a cigar is a tube. Long, skinny tubes, long fat tubes. Or short fat tubes. Each general type has its own name and we will give you them all, remembering that there is considerable variation among manufacturers as to how they are applied.

There are two basic elements when it comes to choosing shape: taste and fashion. While the purists insist that it is only flavor that matters (and, in the end, this is true), there is no denying that each of us generates a different impression on ourselves, and others, depending on what size and shape cigar we hold, and what we look like to begin with. A short, very thin panatela gives us a rakish, Eastwood-esqe look. A longer panatela perhaps gives us a more elegant, continental look. And a larger cigar, say a Churchill, might lend a prosperous (or preposterous), Wall Street, old time Daddy Warbucks sort of style. And while I have learned to consider taste and nothing more, I still am known to peer in the mirror, cheroot tightly clenched between teeth, on occasion, especially after I've had a tequila or two and sneer. But I will never forget the words of the lady on the plane. Back in the days when I managed a stock-brokerage branch, returning to Jacksonville after a regional conference, I put a rather large cigar in my mouth just as the plane touched down, in anticipation of getting off. It had been a long flight and I was tired. A moment later, the lady says, "Well! That cigar's bigger than you are!" To which I innocently replied, with a mock look of bewilderment on my face, after glancing down at my knees for a long moment, "No, it's not." I was able - that time - to turn a rather uncomfortable moment into one of amusement (for all but the well-mannered lady). But know that often, you will be measured by the company of the cigars that you keep.

Unusual Shapes

The only significant deviations from this "rule of the tubes" are these: you can taper the tubes and you can combine the tubes. A pyramid has roughly that shape, though elongated, being very narrow at the head (the end you put in your mouth) and gradually becoming very wide at the foot (also called, for all cigars, the tuck); if the pyramid comes to a rounded head, instead of a point, it is called a belicos. A torpedo starts out narrow, gradually flares out to a much wider girth just above the foot, then tapers sharply down again to a narrow foot. A perfecto is like a torpedo, except the bulge is more toward the middle of the cigar. All of these, as you can imagine, are much more difficult to make than your average roll-em-up cylinder, and they command premium prices. Any difference in taste is surely not justified by the much higher prices, though they can be very impressive wands with which to compel your forces. The culebras is quite the gimmick cigar: three thin, usually machine made, cigars are "braided," or twisted together when wet and pliable, then tied with a string. You, when ready, take them apart and smoke each twisted thing individually. Or together with two like-minded friends.

Unusually-shaped cigars, and unusually-sized cigars, are referred to as figurados by the industry.

The Thickness Makes The Difference

A cigar's diameter is measured by it's "ring gauge." In the U.S., and several other enlightened countries, ring is expressed as 64[ths] of an inch: a ring of 32, for example, would mean a cigar ½ inch in diameter. The more barbaric countries use millimeters, which is far more confusing because we do not get to divide by an easy number.

Not only do thicker cigars allow for more complexity in the blend, they tend to smoke with more authority. The fire is bigger. More logs are burning at the same time. They produce more and heavier smoke with each pull of the mouth. And so they are often considered to be the complex, old red wines - the barolos - of the cigar business, and are favored, most often, by the more experienced smokers, and by those who naturally like more robust things, or who have dampened their taste buds by repeatedly inserting the lit end of the cigar in their mouths. They also tend to smoke slower and therefore last longer for given length, than skinnier cigars, since less length is consumed with each puff. Or so the party line goes. But remember, as Heinlein said, "Climate is what we expect, weather is what we get." I've had many big, thick, macho looking cigars - even light brown ones - that smoked bland and thin. And just as many panatelas - very thin cigars - that were powerful and complex. So thickness is merely one more element that goes into overall quality and flavor. But girth does give the opportunity for more different types of filler, and more filler, period. Properly executed, these are the resonant old kings of the forest, true symphonies of smoke, compared to their thinner, quartet-like brethren. Sample them with care, especially if you are new to the hobby. The taste will grow on you as your palate develops, but may be overpowering at first. Not only are they heavier, but cost more, too, requiring more extra filler, and time in construction, than you might think.

Standard Shapes

What follows is a listing of the more frequently encountered generic size-names for cigars. Yes, there are tons more, and I know that you were hoping for a Spanish lesson. But all of them - including the common ones mentioned here - are used so loosely by the makers as to be nearly useless as a guide to size. Useless, that is, if you demand more precision than a nonchalant large, medium, or small, which is about as accurate as these come in modern usage.

Much better to gauge a cigar by the numbers: in the civilized countries, they are given like this: "7.5x44," which means 7.5 inches long, and 44/64^{ths} of an inch in diameter. 44/64^{ths} is near enough to 2/3^{rds} of an inch across. You'll catch on quick, I promise. Then just use the old names for fun, or to impress and bewilder your tobacconist.

Shape Name	Typical Size
Double Corona	7.5x50
Churchill	7x47
Corona Grande/Gorda	6x46
Robusto	5.5x50
Rothschild	4.5x50
Lonsdale	6.5x42
Corona	5.5x42
Petite Corona	4.5x42
Panatela	4 to 7x37
Cigarillo	4x26

Again, these are the more common names. And no, you don't need me to know that a gigante is a big cigar, but the as-often encountered diademas can be a mystery. 9x50 tells no lies. And who knows what a Presidente might be? Besides, hardly anyone uses the old names much anymore, bastardized or not. At the moment, a Villar y Villar churchill glows in my ashtray. Except it's not a chuchill, it's a valentino. They call their rothchild a robusto and their corona a remedio. They smoke great, but you better look at the pictures in the catalog, or at the numbers.

A few words on some of the common sizes, using the names since numbers can be so cold.

The first thing is that the really big cigars - like the double coronas, or churchills - can create an impression in today's world, even in the hands of a large man, which is distinct and not altogether positive. The tour girl in Venice, for instance, would call me "the big boss from America" whenever I'd light one of these babies up. The other thing is that, besides being full of flavor, they take awhile to smoke. So be sure to mark off your calendar before you shake one loose from its cellophane. These cigars, when well made, are sublime. But I have noticed, even with the better makes, that there seem to be a higher percentage of construction flaws in the larger sizes, maybe because more material means more potential for error. And, with all that material, goes a very high price.

Robustos and Rothschilds are nearly the same cigar, but for an inch or so in length. The first name is more descriptive, since these fellows are meant to deliver great flavor, but be smokeable in a reasonable stretch of time, like after lunch before dashing back to the office. The Rothschild moniker apparently comes from the request of a certain British banker, who in the late 19th century had custom-made a very short version of the double corona, to cut down on his time out of the vault, and away from the tuppence.

The Lonsdale, as you can see, is really a stretch corona, and, like the Rothschild, takes its name from the request of a turn of the century English fellow, this time the Earl of Lonsdale. Not only was the Earl rewarded with an in-your-mouth memorial, but the Cuban maker of which he made the request actually put his picture on the box, and continued to do so for a very long time. Beats the heck out of Wheaties, what?

The corona sizes probably come in as my all-time favorite shape-sizes. With ample ring for a good complexity of flavor, they are short enough, and burn quickly enough (due to the medium ring), that my secretary doesn't have to book an appointment whenever I want to smoke one. These cigars also tend to be more modestly priced and, cheap, time-miserly bastard that I am, I 'd rather have more boxes than fewer, bigger cigars for the same money - especially since I can get back to work quicker. And yes, I own my office building, and no, my employees won't let me smoke there! Actually, it is the effect of stale cigar smoke lingering in the air on my financial planning clients that I fear. But that is the stuff of another chapter. For me, the coronas seem to be the best all-around sizes.

For those of you counting, I lit that Villar y Villar churchill half an hour ago, and we are almost to half-time. And I am a quick smoker, which means I puff a lot.

Now we get to the much-maligned panatela, a name describing thin cigars of varying lengths. The two complaints are these: the cigars are too thin to allow much range of filler, and hence can be bland; and the small diameter also increases the odds of a plug. The first is not true in my experience. When the right filler blend is used, these babies can be powerful, rich, and thoroughly enjoyable. They also look cool as can be and are one of my favorite shapes. They tend to smoke fast, whatever the length, because of the small caliber fire, and to be comparatively reasonably priced, 'cause they don't take much tobacco to make. I have noticed a high incidence of plugs in them, regardless of price or maker. But even with more than a few bad ones, they are cheap enough that your average cost is still pretty good. Try some.

Cigarillos are the smallest of the small, short, and with rings less than half an inch - sometimes a lot less. They smoke fast and usually don't pack too much punch, flavorwise. Unlike a lot of panatelas, these seem mostly to be machine made, and plugging is a persistent problem. They are cheap, though, are O.K. when you want to smoke, but can only spare a few moments. But don't expect too much, please. Often you can get them in tins of 10 at the drugstore, from big brands like Punch and Macadudo.

There you have it! You have successfully endured cigar anatomy 102 and are ready to enter our student exchange program, and have a look at the steaming tropical paradises that produce our favorite delight. Or for the unmarried or under 30, your second favorite delight. Bring a helmet against the occasional guerrilla and you'll be happier if you tote your own toilet paper, as well. A shovel might not hurt, either, since you may prefer a latrine of your own crafting to most of those you find there. Crank up Buffet's <u>Everybody's Got A Cousin In Miami</u>, and hop on de leettle plane!

CHAPTER FIVE

Cigar Countries...
The Lair Of The Beast

Why Country Of Origin Is Now Less Important

Once upon a time, if you bought a Dominican, by golly, what you got when you fired it up was a Dominican. Made completely from Dominican tobacco, except maybe for the wrapper, and tasting that way! There were identifiable differences between brands, to be sure, but each country had its own distinct signature taste coming from the predominant flavor of the tobacco grown there. Alas, the days when one could, blindfolded, magically reveal the fatherland of a given smoke by taste test only are, for the most part, gone, especially for many of the higher-end cigars. Blending is all the rage and I guess it should be, since in the hands of a master it opens up new worlds of cigar experience possibilities.

Consider, from a recent C.A. testing, some of the cigars near the top of the ranking. The Jamaican Macanudo has filler from Mexico and the Dominican Republic (D.R.), binder from Mexico, and Connecticut (that's in the U.S.) wrapper. Nothing from Jamaica. The Honduran Astral gets filler from Nicaragua and the D.R., D.R. binder, and Ecuadorian wrapper. No Honduran tobacco. Contrast this with the simple purity of Fuente's Opus X, which is a clear Dominican, using

D.R. tobacco through and through. And while Fuente does stoop to using non-D.R. wrappers for cigars farther down the quality line, they are all otherwise completely Dominican that I have seen. This is how it is for every Cuban I have encountered - not a drop of capitalist-pig tobacco in 'em, every leaf being grown in the red earth of Cuba ("I'll always be hungry again?"). And I love them that way. Of course, Cuba does also export "raw" tobacco, and not all offshore makers are as faithful to the revolution, and may incorporate non-Cuban leaf and, goodness, even paper! Especially, you must vatch ze Dutch!

So know that the modern high-end cigar can be a hotbed of multinational perdition. And about the only way I know of to find out what countries are included in a given cigar is to check the C.A. taste reports. If you can find the cigar you're interested in somewhere in a review. And if the blend has not changed since it was reported for the review.

Fortunately, bottom-fishing guys like me have an easier time of it, since it is almost certain that most down-scale brand cigars, and probably all bundle cigars - except, perhaps, true seconds, if you can find them - are made nearly entirely from tobacco grown in the country where they are made.

And, by cracky, I like it that way. I want to be able to tell from a cigar's green card if a relationship might be possible, and save the cost of dinner on those I could not possibly want to smoke. My favorite countries, in order, are Cuba, Honduras, and Nicaragua. Again, this is because I like rich, heavy, flavorful cigars, and this is what I get from them. But I will try and be objective as we tour the Caribbean. You may prefer Jamaica's cigars to Marley's music (and back to your counting, Crachett!); I feel the other way. Something for everyone in Montego Bay. And, though Royal Jamaicas were a favorite of my youth and I was crushed to learn that the factory moved to the D.R. in '89; they no longer sing as sweetly to me now.

Anyway, off on the tour. Get on the raft and don't forget to bail. And, remember, no wandering off in the jungle! We'll take the countries in more or less order of importance on the world scene, and not in order of my own preference. Though I suspect my opinions will be clear enough. When we talk about a country, we're mostly concerned with the overall taste and properties of the tobacco grown there. Oh, we may touch on the importance of a given country's cigar industry on the world market. But since manufacturing expertise is now more or less fungible - you can set up a quality cigar making operation nearly anywhere now, even on the streets of Coconut Grove, and blend yourself into oblivion - it is a country's characteristic tobacco flavor that seems to matter. And here we are talking about the tobacco that makes the meat of the cigar, as well as locally grown wrapper, having covered the important wrapper-specialty regions already.

The Four Jaguars

Cuba

Of course, we must start with the true motherland of fine cigars, the once and future economic powerhouse of Cuba. I did not taste Cuban tobacco until rather late in my smoking career, in Hong Kong in 1987. It was love at first bite, though I have consorted with the Cubans only infrequently since then, since the only legal way for a U.S. citizen to do so is to both obtain <u>and</u> smoke them abroad. We'll talk more about the dynamic of this forbidden fruit a little later on. Now we'll just focus on the overall attributes of the fine tobacco from this lovely land. I say lovely because I've seen pictures and ads, and who can forget those scenes from Godfather II, even though they were probably filmed in Alabama. Jeeze, visas are only granted to academics and journalists, but maybe this book will be my ticket to one, and I can go and get those pictures of Cuban women I promised you in the first chapter. Though as a practical matter, any U.S. citizen can get easily in, if only she will go to another country first, then on to Havana. The Cuban customs officials, loving, these days, dollars over rhetoric, simply smile and stamp a blank piece of paper instead of your passport! I've heard that they actually set up special lines for Americans. They'll even take reservations at the Havana Marina, for those who prefer a more leisurely route. It is a wacky world.

Without question, in the minds of the majority who have sampled it, Cuba produces the finest cigar tobacco in the world. Rich, robust, heavy with character and nuance, or delicate yet still deep, the Cuban produce is naturally the finest in the world. Conditions there - climate and soil composition - are naturally ideal. I stress the natural since, like France's finest wine vintage regions, the area seems to be just perfect the way God made it for growing stogie leaf. Inroads have, over the decades, been made in other countries, just as other wonderful wine growing regions - notably California - have been developed this century by the hand of man. In wine, some areas now equal and even surpass the French throne. But not yet, in my opinion, for Cuba. Very close indeed, but no cigar. Despite years of soil mismanagement under the Communists, Cuban leaf still manages to reign supreme. But be careful, the Hondurans, Nicaraguans, and Dominicans are coming close on the heals of the king. And behind them, with the dollars from the worldwide cigar boom on the wind, a host of others. Cuba must - has, I think - pick up the pace.

Cuban tobacco is generally thought of as being very heavy and powerful, wonderful and complex. And for many of us, this is what makes for the best cigars. But realize that blending - in any country - can make for cigars which are mild and understated, almost dainty. Except that when such are made in Cuba - or outside with part Cuban tobacco - the rich signature taste still softly sings through, and makes them wonderful, and still without peer in their class.

Not that garbage cigars, crudely made and using inferior tobacco, are not made in Cuba. They are and will be, for lower price points, and to fill the hastily printed boxes of the counterfeits. But forgive me if I find even the garbage from

Cuba to be often very good, and sometimes better than the
best from other nations. Call me a Cubophile, at least in the
style of Kennedy, if you must.

Dominican Republic

Comprising very roughly one half of the Caribbean island of Hispanolia, which it shares with Haiti, the D.R. is
now arguably the most important cigar producing nation in
the world. Nearly half of the cigars consumed in the U.S.
come from here, the industry is well established, and growing with a vengeance, and many major brands - like Fuente
and Partagas - are entrenched in the market and extremely
well regarded. In recent years non-Cuban cigars - especially
from the D.R. - have made significant inroads against the
Cubans in the European markets as well.

While long considered to be a producer of quality filler
tobacco only, Dominica is now growing a lot of binder and
wrapper as well, and exporting a lot of "clear" Dominicans.

Enjoying cigars from this land has always been a chal-
lenge for me, since I find most of them to taste mild and
rather subdued. Even those regarded as heavily and full
flavored - like the Fuente Hemmingway - for me just approach the fullness that I routinely taste in even mediocre
Hondurans, Nicaraguans, and Cubans. Once again, do not
go by me entirely, since I am clearly in the minority - at least
in the U.S. - on this one. Cigars are so subjective a delight
that each of us really needs to do a bit of exploratory work to
find what suits us best.

It is an interesting aside that Haiti, just spitting distance
from the D.R. and in fact sitting on the same piece of rock,
has virtually no cigar industry of note, proving once again
that Voodoo is no substitute for capitalism.

Honduras

This Mayan homeland, like the D.R., became of great
interest in the '60's to the expatriated Cuban cigar kings as
they scoured the Caribbean, seeking new fields to till. In

Honduras, it is said that they found conditions most similar to those they left behind in Cuba and many new kingdoms were carved. Today, this country is the world's second largest producer, and sells about two-thirds as many cigars in the U.S. as does the D.R.

It is also said that the tobacco produced in this country is most similar to the Cuban output, and I enthusiastically agree. Honduran leaf is rich, flavorful, and strong in a complex way, and for my mouth, most of the best non-Cuban cigars are made here. Also, for the penny-wise, the bundle output is prodigious and often quite inexpensive. You can even get decent brand stuff from here - like most of Villizon's Bances line - for under a buck a piece at retail.

And while almost all of this - heavenly tobacco and good prices - is shared by its neighbor to the south, Nicaragua, the lack of political upheaval has allowed a smoother development of Honduras' cigar industry. But the folks from south of the border are catching up fast. You never sausage a cigar! Keep screaming kids! Only 216 miles to Pedro!

Nicaragua

Another country with near-perfect cigar growing regions, especially those close to the Honduran border. As mentioned above, the time of the Sandinistas just about killed the cigar industry here, with fields and factories actually burned to the ground - an interesting variation on the time-honored technique of jungle agriculture called "slash and burn." Excellent and well loved old brands like Joyo de Nicaragua virtually disappeared. Now, on the wind of democracy, the business has finally recovered, and wonderful product from this troubled land is on the market again. Like Honduras, and maybe even more so, this tobacco is very Cuban-like: rich, strong, packed with flavor and subtlety. While, like for all countries, the best - and sometimes the no-so-best - is quite expensive, there is great value in bundles and boxes on very good quality Nicaraguan cigars, though on the whole I still seem to be doing better with the Hondurans. Search them out and check them out.

Jaguar Kittens, a Canary, and Tigers, Too!

Mexico

Mexico's been exporting more than labor these days. In fact, they've been sending us cigars for quite a long time now, though the pace has picked up with demand as it has for virtually all cigar making countries. Mexico's flagship brand has long been Te-Amo, but of course there has now been an explosion of premium and super premium brands. None have yet impressed me very much, though I admittedly don't go to the Mexican counter very often to see what's popped up. Mexican tobacco has a reputation for being strong, without much range or flavor, more of a beef jerky than a prime rib, and has always tasted that way to me. The common Maduro wrappers don't help this much. But quality is said to be rapidly improving and you may want to give one or two a try. This may be due, in part, to a recent change in Mexican law, no longer requiring cigars to be made "puro"...Spanish for "clear," or entirely of (in this case) Mexican tobacco. You may now put Heinz ketchup on your refried beans. So try. Especially if your kids force a stop at a certain miniature theme park on I-95 in South Carolina, and you buy a sombrero. Just don't say that you're "smoking with Pedro tonight," or the DEA may come looking for you.

Jamaica

For my money, this is the last "real" cigar making country on the tour. The long-famous Macanudos are made here, though they don't use much Jamaican tobacco, as well as other established brands. The island's contribution to the maw of cigardom seems to come more from rolling than from growing. Since this makes the cigars tough to classify by the soil, I'll just say that what I've had from here is good, though a bit on the light side. But they be smokin', Mon. Stir it up.

Philippines

And off to the shark-infested waters of Subic Bay and the fields of the post-Marcos Philippines. Besides the constant unearthing of woman's shoes as they till the soil, tobacco grows well here. Unfortunately, to me, it tastes more like shoes. Pretty on the outside, but hot, smelly, and unappetizing on the inside. For most of us. But bad enough that I suggest you skip it.

Canary Islands

Proximity to Spain drew many of Cuba's cigar lords in the wake of Castro (bet that strikes a chord in Miami, "the wake of Castro..."), but the tobacco grown on these rocks tastes like magma. Some are still made here, mostly with Caribbean tobacco. To me they taste light and thin. I'd still skip them, since better stuff just gushes closer to home.

Brazil

Who knows what lurks in the jungles of this, South America's largest and most mysterious country. Although cigars have been made here for years, the decent cigar industry is still in it's infancy. So at this point Brazil gets a resounding "no comment," with best hopes for the future. Try 'em from time to time if you like and smoke history in the making. Just remember how bloody history has been...

China

Call this one the great red hope, the last bastion of Communism that has any chance of surviving, though it's likely survival is clearly the result of the adoption of free market reforms. Spurring the interesting question, "if a politico uses his graft money to set up a business, is he still a communist?" But better is this one from the Car Talk Brothers: "If a man speaks and a woman doesn't hear him, is he still wrong?" We digress. More is known about Silkworm missiles than about Chinese cigars, and though it seems some have been hitting the market, I have yet to see any. Maybe because I don't spend much time in the textile importing districts. Given the vast agricultural acreage and the millennia-long mercantile expertise of the Chinese people, yoked or otherwise, I think that it is only a matter of time. The sleeping giant has awoken, demanding coffee and ginseng, and, I think, soon, cigars.

Columbia!

For goodness sake, it looks like the whole world's trying to cash in on the cigar craze. I went surfing last night to develop material for the Cigars on the 'Net chapter and found - would you believe it? - cigars offered from a forgotten valley in Columbia, where they have been made for centuries, which were purported on the Web page to be better even than Cuban Cohibas! At the bargain price of only $140 the box of 25! And yes! They do take credit cards! Just fax your Mastercard number to our unassuming little, impoverished, druglord-ravaged village, and we will process, with complete security, through the Banco de Bogata! We don't know how long we can keep this up, the bullets are whizzing! And just look at that hand-crafted-by-the-Mayan-pyramids junglewood box! Hurry, senor! Ah, they got my brother! You see, my brother dies for your gringo cigars! You better buy some!

Sadly, I have never sampled these undiscovered gems from the Colombian jungle and, at these prices, with this come-on, I'm not likely to any time soon, so the taste of Colombian tobacco is still a mystery to me.

Stay tuned for more fast breaking news from the Net, and lots of cool sights. Not only is there much to amuse, like this last piece, but lots of useful stuff, too.

Anyway, there you have it, our tour is at an end. While we have emphasized the "four jaguars" of the Caribbean - Cuba, D.R., Honduras, and the resurrected Nicaragua, don't forget the hungry kittens prowling the jungles. Please remember that you will be processed through customs in a moment and that anything left on the boat will be confiscated and auctioned to augment the U.S. Treasury.

Chapter Six

Where to Find 'Em, How to Buy 'Em Right

Primary sources are that great smelling, cozy shop around the corner, that sells cigars and all kinds of other neat stuff, and the mail order houses, both the true discounters, and the débutantes. We'll talk about the advantages of each and give you some opinions - and contact info - on particular mail order vendors. Then there are the folk on the fringe, like drinking establishments, drug and liquor stores (which have some great stuff these days), sources you see when you travel out of the country, and the fellow who approaches you in an ally - or says he got your name from a buddy at the country club - saying "Heh, meester, want to buy some Cubans?" - to which the appropriate response always should be, "How fast can they pick apples?" No disrespect to Cuban-Americans, or to Cuban-Cubans, for that matter. I just thought it was funny, what with NAFTA, and all that cheap labor sloshing around, and all. Anyway, we will give you invaluable insight, unavailable elsewhere, on these sources, as well.

Traditional Sources

Tobacconists

These are the salt of the earth of the cigar business, both the chain shops like Tinder Box, and the singles, like the wonderfully-named Politically Incorrect Tobacco & Gifts in L.A.

No, we won't give you a nationwide directory of shops - or clubs and cigar friendly restaurants, for that matter - at the end of the book, like most of the other cigar books do. I know it looks nice, fills up some pages, and <u>seems</u> like it would be awfully useful. But if you're like me, you won't ever use it. You'll probably forget the damn book when you travel, and even if you don't, you won't have any time to hunt down shops on unknown streets when you get there, anyway. Bring your cigars with you, or check the yellow pages or the concierge when you get there. As for your home turf, use the phone book, and I will forget that you asked such a question.

Shops are neat. The atmosphere is usually quite nice and they are full of future friends who share your enthusiasm, or at least are sympathetic to your passion. Often - but not always, and less and less as shops spring up - the person behind the counter is very knowledgeable, and can be of great help in guiding you. If not, subtly suggest they read this book. Shops are chock full of cigar and pipe paraphernalia, and often have nice selections of quality gifts, high end pens, stuff like that. From a smoking standpoint, the biggest advantage - besides the advice of the tobacconist - is that you get to see, feel, and smell the merchandise before you buy, and to buy just one of each that appeals to see if you like it. Heck, they often have furniture and ashtrays set up, so you can socialize while you sample. They are very nice places to hang out and get a feeling for what your preferences might be.

So the upside is congenial atmosphere, see and touch, buy just one, and plenty of neat "add on sale" toys. The downside is less-than-unlimited selection and slightly-higher prices. The little guys are finding it harder and harder to get inventory, what's here today is often gone tomorrow as they scramble for anything to fill the shelves, and storage space is limited to humidor size to begin with. And still they have trouble keeping them full. Higher prices come from having to cover overhead with limited volume, and simply, because customers will pay it. If they don't, it probably won't be there tomorrow. And who can blame the merchant for charging whatever the market will bear, especially with the trouble he goes through to fill the shelves in the first place?

Sad to say, storage conditions in shops vary considerably. What you want is a walk-in humidor, where the mist virtually billows, and the cigars are obviously fresh. Or at least cabinet humidors that are properly maintained. Cigars - as we will see in greater detail when we talk about home storage - should be kept at about 70 degrees Fahrenheit, in air that is about 70% relative humidity. If you can see the gauges, all the better, but you can usually tell if the air is "wet." In any event, a "fresh" cigar should be resilient, slightly pliable, and obviously, without wrapper cracks. When we say fresh, we mean not necessarily new, but well kept; in fact, cigars improve with age for a long time before heading south, the best are aged for a year or more before leaving the factory, and all are nearly unsmokable when first finished; if you get a batch that tastes "green" and you suspect inadequate aging at the factory, try "laying them down" for awhile in your humidor - they should get a lot better. Although the other books advise against this as bad cigar etiquette, a gentle squeeze, or roll between the fingers, should give a good idea of freshness in the store, even through cellophane. Without "cello," even better, since you can both feel and smell for freshness. Even in the best shops, you may find cigars that are stale, perhaps because they have been there long (not such a problem anymore!), perhaps in a section of the humidor that receives poor circulation. In the worst shops - both old and new - you'll find some dry as dust, shoved in a showcase, unloved and unsmoked. Be careful when you see this, because cigars even fresh off the truck have a very short shelf life when stored this way. I've even seen "humidors" where one glass wall was exposed to the full Florida sun (in fact the humidor itself was part of the storefront, which faced south), and buckets of water were set on the floor to overcome the effects of the heat. Literal buckets. Sadly, they did not, the cigars were husks and the shop is no longer in business.

Fortunately, most shops are well-maintained, very congenial, and sport knowledgeable and helpful staff. They are great places to get the lay of cigarland.

Mail Order Houses

The right ones of these have become the mainstay of serious smokers, especially those of us that smoke a few or more each day. Here you can get very good stuff at very good prices - in some cases even cheaper than ten years ago! - if you are willing to sample sight unseen, and try a bundle or a box instead of just one. Believe me, if you smoke a lot, this is still cheaper - even if you occasionally toss or give away a bundle or box of "bad ones" - than shopping "retail."

First, we have to separate the true discounters from the fast buck Johnny-come-latelys, whose slick catalogs often taste better than the overpriced cigars they tout. And they are legion. All over the Net. All over my mailbox. Most of these might be indistinguishable from the real thing, the old players trying to deliver true value. The best way to tell is through experience, having seen them around for awhile, and having sampled their wares and service. Not that some fine merchants may not be developing now, more interested in the long term, in providing quality at a fair price, and building a customer base. Without guidance, you must rely on trial and error, as I have. Here are some I've dealt with in the past, with favorable results. Where possible, I've collected comprehensive data, mostly off the Web. Where not, I give you what I know.

The first is <u>Thompson & Co.</u>, out of Tampa. I've been getting their catalogs for years and have bought more than a few times. Selection is often good and they often run "deals" on big lots of stuff they've been able to acquire on good terms. I've found prices higher than elsewhere in the mail-order universe, but generally better than in the shops. And remember that you can usually avoid sales tax on mail order if you order out of your state, and if the vendor doesn't have

operations in your state. The staff at Thompson's is friendly and they seem to be small enough that you'll get the same person (who may even remember you!) more often than not.
Thompson & Co., Established 1915.
Phone: 800-237-2559
Customer Service: 813-243-6172
Fax: 813-882-4605
5401 Hangar Court, Tampa, FL 33634
Hours: 8a-12a M-F; 9a-6p Sa-Su (EST)
Payment: AmEx, MC, VISA, Disc, DC

Another venerable vendor is Nat Sherman, of New York. Although I've never purchased from them, they are one of the brighter glows in the smoke-filled room, and well worth trying. In fact, Joel, son of Nat, has written a decent book himself (Nat Sherman's A Passion For Cigars, Andrews & McMeel, 1996), which is worth checking out even if he does spend a bit of paper "plugging" his own smokes...just kidding, Joel!
Nat Sherman
Tobacconist to the World for Over 65 Years.
Phone: 800-221-1690
Fax: 212-246-8639
500 Fifth Avenue, New York, NY 10110
Payment: AmEx, MC, Visa, DC, Check, MO

Another house I've had good luck with in the past is Holt's, finding product in stock at generally fair prices. They've been around since 1898.
Holt's Cigar Company
FREE 72 page, color catalogue.
800-523-1641
1522 Walnut Street
Philadelphia, PA 19102
215-732-8500

Of course, the great, great granddaddy of them all is Lew Rothman of J.R. Tobacco, arguably the biggest retailer of cigars in the world. I've been buying from J.R. for years and years, always with good result. The cigar story vignettes in

the catalogs have kept me in stitches for as long as I can
remember, and value delivered is absolutely second to none.
Prices are excellent - I've been able to buy Villizon product
from J.R. at the same or lower cost than wholesale from
Villizon direct, and still get it from J.R. long after Villizon
became interminably "backordered" - and some values are
truly beyond belief, like the Mocha Hondurans I'm currently
ordering by the carload. J.R.'s volume is tremendous, and
allows them to cut deals extro'dinaire with the makers. It
would not surprise me to find that they owned more than a
few factories. But beyond this, the company truly seems to
care about delivering fair value and keeping prices down.
Like so many others, they could have made a mint (all right,
a third mint to go with the two they're making anyway) during the current cigar boom, jacking prices, hoarding product, and riding the wave. To their credit, and probably to
their long term business sense, they have not. Strongly and
absolutely recommended, across all product lines. Search
and try the bundle deals, especially those held out as special
buys, where "I had to buy the town but I got these babies for
a short song...and I can't sing!" (I made this one up), or "They
had over 500,000 excellent cigars already made and season-
ing, but they didn't have any bands or boxes to pack the
cigars in! Jackpot! This is my kind of deal and boy did I buy
this stuff right." (quote from Lew in the current catalog).

JR Tobacco of America
Is Now In A Position
To Accept New Customers
1515 East Broad Street
Statesville, North Carolina 28677
Philadelphia, PA 19102
1-800-JR-CIGAR (800-572-4427)
Fax 1-800-4-JR-FAXX (800-457-3299)

I left that bit of hype in from the cut & pasted Web
data to give you a feeling for what this company's culture is
like. And one more quote: "...and a lot of the cigars today
are nothing but real junk in fancy boxes...You see ads in

Cigar Aficionado and Smoke Magazine of absolutely gorgeous cigars, along with a bunch of bull**** copy about how some family has been making these things in their basement for a hundred years. Then you run out and end up paying five or ten dollars for a cigar that's almost entirely composed of "green" trash tobacco, wrapped in some mangy Indonesian wrapper...give me a break...Can you imagine what would happen if JR sent you a catalog with pictures of great big juicy cigars with beautiful oily wrappers, and then shipped you a bunch of bleached out cigars ¼ the size of the picture you saw? Well, don't worry. When you buy Lew's Smokers [a house bundle brand at about $1.00/cigar], you're gonna get the exact same ugly cigars you see on this page."

Once again, there are no doubt many other fine and long standing cigar mail order discounters, and I apologize if I have missed them, either because they never mailed me, or because I never came across them in the "literature." If you know of others that have pleased you, super, use them, and let me know for future editions of this book. If not, you will do well with those mentioned above, especially the cornucopia of cigars that is J.R. And believe me, my enthusiasm for the J.R. operation is completely unsolicited by them, and, sadly, unpaid. Though I am hoping to tempt Lew into writing a forward for the book, that lies in the future, and my satisfaction with them is a matter of historical record.

Drugstores

Drugstores -especially the major chains have been in the cigar business for a while, and often have some good-quality stuff. Most often this is to be found in the tobacco section on an aisle. In addition to the overwhelming selection of cellophane-wrapped-box machine made product, there is usually a selection of "private-brand" handmade cigars from at least several important countries. Much of it is good, all of it convenient. Of course, given the environment, do not expect knowledgeable staff.

The situation is similar for big discount chains, like Wal-Mart and K-Mart.

Liquor Stores

Liquor stores seem to have lately gotten into the cigar business in a big way, especially the larger chain stores. They often sport tobacconist-grade humidors, a selection of toys, and staff who at least knows the rudiments of good cigars-man-ship. While the buyers who actually pick the product to stock the humidors have not been at it long - and this is occasionally reflected in the wide selection - they are apparently catching on fast.

Strategies For A Tight Market

So. Want to spare yourself buying "green garbage" at $10 a pop? Tired of endless shopping and sampling at the cigar counter, as the old inventory (where you found suitable cigars) is flushed out, and entirely new (and unknown) stuff is flushed in? Heard "sorry, they're on backorder, don't know when they'll be in" too many times?

Well, sadly, the secret now is simply striking when the cigar is hot. Find what you like, at what you think is a fair price. Pay what you want, but remember that very good cigars - if you don't insist on gigantes - can still be had for well under a buck apiece, and that truly great stuff is around for about $2 or so. Don't buy into the haze that you gotta pay $5, $10, or, like the poor fellow in the shop in Nassau, $50 for a single cigar. Be cheap, be smart. Buy a "power smoke" for the band if you must, but use the band over and over on your sensible smokes, just like you do with that Chevis bottle you've had since 1982. Enough. It's your money.

Finding what you like, buy all you can get. We'll show you how to store them nicely and cost effectively in just one jiffy. If in a shop, buy all the boxes or bundles. If the clerk balks, explain that the cigars will be sold anyway, and selling them now increases his turnover and profit. And also encourages other customers to buy more, also bumping profit. Explain that you don't have this problem at other shops. If still they seek to limit you, go back the next day - and the next - and get the rest. Send wife, boyfriend, secretary, whatever, to save your valuable time, and to obtain them all. But get them all, because if you don't, I will! It's a jungle, with every sucker for himself. For the suckers who don't read this book, there'll be plenty of the $5 cigars left, anyway.

At the mail order houses, the strategy is similar and easier - just a phone call. Some will sell you all you want. Some have started to ration. J.R., for instance, will limit you to four boxes/bundles of a particular item per order, with an absolute limit on the total, probably in an attempt to keep the items offered in the catalog in stock for a reasonable period of time. Maybe so, Lew, but it still sounds like a vodka line in old Moscow to me! Sometimes the phone clerk can be cajoled into increasing your allotment. In not, call and reorder, day after day, until your little treasure chest is bursting. Enlist your bowling buddies and your coworkers if you must, but find a way to buy until sated. By the way, there is no limit if you actually visit a J.R. shop, like the one on I-95 in North Carolina I pass a couple times a year. I filled my trunk last time I was there.

This sounds brutal, I know, smacking of a horde mentality and disregard for other brothers and sisters in smoke. But trust me, it is the only way. Ignore it and you destine yourself to endless cycles of sample, buy, toss what you don't like, and sample again when you've smoked the two boxes they "let you have." Try to remember that the customer - not the merchant - is king, the shortage is in many ways a sham, and, like Doritos, they will make more. Just takes, like corn, seed, soil, and sun.

A final word: beware backorders. Like a forgotten good 'till canceled order for stock, these things have a tendency to be filled only after you have completely forgotten about them and no longer want the stuff. And, unlike for a stock GTC, the price may not be fixed in advance. So beware and order accordingly. Or just shop elsewhere if they don't have what you want and can't assure a reasonable timeframe.

The Man On The Street: le Count de Counter-feet

This traffic seems to be pretty much limited to cigars represented as Cubans, sold this way because they are illegal in the U.S. Now I don't have a big moral problem with Cuban cigars, as you may have surmised. It think the embargo is silly and ineffective. But you don't care about my geopolitical views. But if you decide to get your adrenaline all pumped up to break the law, at least make sure that you have broken it, and for good product.

And, for the most part, these black marketeers are hawking shoddy stuff, billed as the real thing. True, there are some genuine Cuban brands to be had on the street, but most often they are counterfeits, and in the worse cases, not even Cuban.

Here's one example. After a 1996 Jaguars game in Jacksonville, I was headed up to Boston on business. Ironically, my connection was in Charlotte, and the plane was loaded with dejected Panthers fans. Although I never removed my Jags hat, I struck up a conversation with my Charlottean seat mate in first class, and we became friends. Turned out he was a cigar fan and had a "connection" who got him "Cubans" through the mail. I've forgotten what brand he said they were supposed to be, but he was paying something like $10 apiece for them. He promised to send me one, to which I looked forward with great relish. Sad to say, on arrival, the cigar turned out to be an unaged sandwich, probably made in a garage in Guatemala, with tobacco they grew out back where they dump the used oil. I never had the heart to tell him, but this guy was paying $10 for $0.25 smokes. But he was happy!

Another case is the Jacksonville pharmaceutical salesman I told you about, who was referred to me by one of my doctor clients. Code-named "The Lone Ranger," this Cuban fellow told me he had Montecristos and Cohibas, at something like $250 a box. Said his contact had no trouble smuggling them in, since "she just got in line where she saw a Cuban customs official, who would look the other way because he knew the money was going to the poor folks back home." Or some rubbish. After lunch, I bought a box marked Cohiba Lanceros. Should have known better, but I did. Although made from Cuban leaf and pretty good because of it, the cigars turned out to be obvious fakes. Fakes available on every street corner in Havana, to be sure, but fakes still, worth maybe $30/box including the smuggling risk.

So, unless your palate and eye are very well tuned, I'd stay away from this source. Most of the time the stuff is junk. As it is so easy to get caught up in the mystery of it all, that whatever cigar judgment you do have just goes up in smoke, and, like me, you buy trash and pay for lunch!

Spotting Counterfeits

This should be no mystery, since most of the bogus stuff is of obvious inferior manufacture. That goes for the packaging as well as the cigars. By now, you should have a good feeling for what a quality cigar looks like. Smooth, unblemished, oily wrapper with a quality of depth to it. All long filler. No books in the construction. Cigars are an important export for Cuba, and the major brands are subject to pretty rigid quality control. They look like the premium product they are. And so does the packaging. Crisp, vivid printed colors on the bands and boxes. Everything sharply lined up. Bands all lined up and tight on each cigar. Ribbons in the box and cello - if they come with it - just so. The bogus boxes often have fuzzy printing, with labels haphazardly slapped on the boxes. Printing of lower quality, using poorer paper. The tax seal, however - the official paper label glued on the box, which must be broken to open the box - may be stolen and real. And the cigars themselves are obviously second rate. Usually made of inferior, though Cuban, tobacco, they have a shoddy appearance. The Cohibas mentioned above, for instance, bled short filler as soon as I bit off the end.

The best test is the same yardstick you would apply to any cigar. With the "Cubans" likely to be offered to you, if they don't look like premiums, they probably ain't real. If still tempted, at least sample just one before deciding. And try not to get drawn in by the cloak and dagger mystique.

I have not seen any counterfeit product made to look like non-Cuban premiums, though with the prices these things are bringing, I think that it is just a matter of time. So inspect. While your best assurance is still gotten by buying from a recognized dealer, this stuff, if and when it appears, will probably creep into his stock. Especially if it is a smaller outlet, the wholesale buyer is not an expert, and becomes swayed by a pickup truck full of ½ price Macanudos in these times of short supply and empty shelves.

As I edit this, I must tell you that it has appeared! A tobacconist friend of mine tells me she bought a big order of brand Dominicans because the price was right, only to find they were bogus. And she got them from a big national source mentioned in this book. So beware! We are all one step from chagrin...

Again, caveat smoker. And remember that only a fool would try and counterfeit bundles!

Cigar Clubs, Bars, and Restaurants:
The Call of the Big Smoke

This will be a pretty short section, since I don't hang out in such places much. The first thing is that there has been an explosion of cigar-specific and cigar-friendly establishments across the "fruited plain." Cigar specific places - cigar clubs - are devoted to the activity, encourage smoking, and offer ancillary services, like bars, big screen TV's, and "lockers," or rented drawers in their big humidors, in addition to a social setting teeming with like-minded folks. Many charge dues and are members only places. I'm sure that these are great places, wonderful to pass time and make friends in.

But cigars can be combined with so many other pleasurable activities - golf, the boat, many bars, and on and on, that you need not feel limited to the confines of the reservations.

Cigar-friendly places permit - sometimes only on designated dates, like for smoker nights - the use of cigars without fear of ejection, and an implicit promise that non-smoking patrons will be kept at bay. And this friendliness is like eternal love expanding, as the restaurants sense the change in the market, and seek to maximize their traffic.   Often the smoking area - like the bar in my local country club - will be equipped with a filter to keep the billowing (and the bellowing?) to a minimum. And while many states limit "public" smoking to designated areas, no laws, to my knowledge, yet discriminate against cigars but permit cigarettes, though lots of restaurants still do. When in doubt, politely ask an employee first.   It is also nice to let the unlit cigar dangle from your mouth for a few minutes, to announce your intentions, and see if you spark any vehement comment from your neighbors in the room.   Though, I think, the rules of the house should prevail, if you get a complaint and choose to ignore it. More on this in the etiquette section later.

A new kind of event - the "Big Smoke" type things - have gotten very popular lately, where devotees gather for an evening of fine food, fine wine, and, of course, a cigar or two between courses. I am sure that these are delightful affairs, well worth the cost of the ticket. The bigger ones in major cities usually draw celebrities, and often manufactures will attend and offer samples to promote their brands. If interested, the best sources are the magazines for the bigger events, and local shops and computer billboards for the local stuff. The magazines, like C.A., carry sections listing cigar friendly places, which often sponsor smoker gatherings.

Buying Abroad (or two)

A Breath of Fresh Smoke

When out of the country, you legally have the luxury of shopping for and enjoying Cuban cigars. This is a good thing, because non-Cuban brands are often not available in any great supply in other countries. We'll talk about the wisdom of bringing back to the U.S. in a moment.

While you'll see tons of well priced, good Cubans in the duty free shops of most major airports, most of us want to buy and smoke on the streets of the cities we visit, not at the last minute before we jump on the plane home. Your best advice is, of course, the locals, though you may have trouble explaining the kind of cigars that you are looking for, that Dutch Masters may not, quite, do. If your hotel has a concierge, it is his duty to track one down for you. If not, try and find an informed local who speaks your language. The Pakistani cab driver may know, but not be able to tell. Do beware of venturing off into parts of the city where tourists may not be embraced (or may be embraced and pick-pocketed!). But since the kind of shop with the stuff you're looking for will usually be located in a reasonably upscale part of town, you should be O.K.

Prices vary considerably by country, mostly because of taxes imposed. Canada and the Bahamas I've found to be ridiculously high. An interesting aside is that while the Canadian duty free shops going back into the U.S. stock Cubans, they wont let you buy them! Just how many happy Hungarians shop at the Niagara Falls border before dashing back to the Toronto airport, anyway? The taxes in Canada - on all cigars - were incredible. I found Honduran cigars in shops priced singly for what I could get a whole bundle for in the States. Hong Kong in its pre-Red days was very inexpensive. Italy has fair prices. And so on. Shop when you get there and pay what you feel is reasonable. As a rule of thumb, you should be able to get a good hand-made Cuban brand of corona size cigars for about U.S.$70 for the box of 25. Yes, I know that such a price runs counter to everything you have read so far, but these are <u>Cubans</u> and a special treat. And I have seen such boxes as high as $250 U.S. in the worst countries. Also remember, you smugglers, that the duty free shops in the airports often have excellent prices, since they carry no tax, only excessive mark-up.

The brand choice can be tough, since most of us are unfamiliar with even recognized brands in their Cuban manifestations. Machine made stuff is often offered side by side with handmade, and is often surprisingly good. Of machine mades, I've had good luck with Belinda, less with H. Upmann and Partagas. Of handmades, I've consistently found Partagas to be an excellent buy. Well made and robust, they have pleased in many sizes, from many countries. But look for totalmente a mano, since hecho en Cuba means only made in Cuba, and most brands have extensive lines, from the best super premiums to the lowliest machine made cigarillos. And the boxes all look pretty much the same.

Bringing Cuban Cigars Into the U.S.

This can be a thorny issue. It is illegal. If you are caught, you run the risk of being entered into a database of known smugglers, and being subject to sanctions. Overwhelmingly, when found, the cigars are merely (merely?) confiscated, to be burned (they say...), and you are let to go your not-so-merry-anymore way. It is a joke of a law and seemingly viewed that way by those in the service. But enforce the law they must. I have a Customs officer as a client, who told me of an oriental family that was caught smuggling a large fortune in diamonds - the family wealth - into the U.S. when they immigrated here in 1997. Because the stones were undeclared, they were seized, for good. The irony is, he told me, that there is no duty imposed on such stones, and had they been declared, no tax would have been due! Sad but true and another dent in the deficit...

Back to illicit cigars. If you do decide to bring some back - and I cannot condone such behavior - the risks are extremely slight, but real. Hundreds, probably thousands, do it every day. The vast majority of folks, especially of respectable appearance, go unsearched, with a brief conversation and a look at the Customs tax form. I have never been searched, even before I grew to look respectable. Make your choice and take your chances. I won't tell you to pack the contraband down in the depths of your smelly laundry. Or to remove the bands and put them into an empty Dominican box. And, by the way, I don't think the dogs have been trained to sniff out cigars. Or at least not tell Communist Punch from Honduran Punch.

Just don't put any raw meat in there.

Smoking Mechanics and Other Rituals, Cigar Etiquette, And the First Batch of Toys

The Snobbery of Proper Technique

Got your napkin on your left and your glass on the right? Good. Wouldn't want to upset your delicate sensibilities. If we can not tell dessert spoon from salad fork we are no better than the beasts that we are.

I will tell you the party line on the civilized and accepted techniques of proper cigar handling as far as I know them. Then I will tell you how I do it. But know this. On the non-cigar smoker, any nuance of technique is lost. Even to most cigarette smokers, you are a barbarian, whether you use an 18 karat cutter, toenail clippers, or your teeth to remove the end. Most would rather see you take a cigar enema than smoke the darn thing. I mean they really would rather see it. But don't you let them.

So at best, you will impress only other cigar buffs. At true best, like Cyrano D'Bergerac (please, quiet, I can barely spell in English!) you will impress at least yourself.

Clipping the Head

The refined smoker of cigars removes the head mechanically, which has spawned all sorts of Rabbi jokes. The head, of course, is the end of the cigar meant to go in your mouth, which is covered, for appearance only, by the cap, that round flap of tobacco glued (with safe, harmless, tasteless and smokeless goo, of unknown origin) on at the factory. This must be removed for the passage of smoke. Those brutes among us use our teeth which, after long practice, can be trained to gently nibble the end off, clean and true as gutting a trout. It is important to remove only <u>most</u> of the cap, leaving a thin circle to hold the end of the wrapper together. Cut off the whole thing and, like the Rabbi, you have a mess on your hands, a massive unraveling, and a lot of explaining to do. Though surely God's will is invoked less often for maimed cigars. The object is to remove about 80% of the cap, symmetrically, giving a hole big enough to pass the smoke unimpeded, but leaving enough glued on to hold the cigar together.

Cigar Cutters

There are four classes of popular devices which will do this, any of which will look just dandy dangling from your keychain. We take them in order of effectiveness.

Guillotine

The first, and best, as the French found, is the handy guillotine. This device is really just a guide plate through which a blade (or blades) slides. Open it and you see a hole in the plate. Start to close and the blade moves across the hole, cutting whatever is inserted. The best use two blades, one from one end, one the other, cutting at the same time, and reducing tearing.

Guillotines are best because they cut a clean slice off the end of the cigar, which is what you want. Positioning the opened plate, or frame, over the cigar's cap determines the diameter of the cut, and, hence, how much of the cap you remove. Since the size of the hole is usually quite generous, these can accommodate many different rings, and, as we will see in the repair section, can be used to lop whole sections of the cigar off, when drastic measures are called for.

My double guillotine is a Davidoff Zino, with great, self-sharpening (so they say) blades, and with a frame of about the same quality plastic as found in my Porsche. It is very handy since you can stick a finger into the loops at each end to control each blade, letting you work it - by squeezing it and so sending each blade home at the same time - with one hand, saving the other hand for the cigar. It is a fine instrument, but cost about $70. I have seen very similar designs offered on the market at much lower prices, but haven't yet used one. But I must say, they do look identical. And I will buy one when I lose my Zino, just as I will shop Mustangs when my 130K mile '87 Porsche - bought just before the crash (stock market, wiseguys), if you are paying attention - finally stops driving sweet, and letting me throw it onto the Interstate ramps with almost-complete abandon. But not before. Well, maybe before: I got a ticket for racing coming home from the clubs with my brother early last Saturday morning, so perhaps an SUV looms for me now.

Anyway, I coulda bought five, maybe six, bundles for what that Zino cost.

I haven't yet lost it, by the way, because it <u>always</u> hangs in my humidor. Away from home, I use my teeth. And to nearly all who look, I am just as barbaric as if I had brought my guillotine. I've got enough stuff hanging from my keychain, anyway.

Cigar Scissors

These are really a neat item, scissors designed especially to trim cigar caps. Good ones are not cheap, but can be very impressive. They work about the same way as a double guillotine, except that the blades swing free, without a frame, and that they pivot instead of falling parallel to each other. This last characteristic makes it more important to keep scissors sharp: with a guillotine, pressure is more or less evenly distributed, hitting opposite sides of the cigar as it cuts through, thus holding it in place and reducing the odds of tearing. Scissors apply pressure mostly in the apex of the blades, squeezing the smoke and pinching it on one side. So keep 'em sharp, or you may wind up ripping the head - or more - off, instead of getting a nice clean slice. Or at least twisting and damaging the cigar.

But wouldn't a pair look grand, hanging from a chain around your neck! You can make a grand popping noise by briskly slapping your opened palm against your slightly opened mouth, and sachet around like a sommelier.

The V Cut

This device, looking and working something like a small stapler, is designed to cut a v-shaped wedge out of the end of the cigar, the idea being that by exposing more surface area of filler, draw will be improved. Maybe so, but it makes no difference in actual practice, and a lack of very sharp blades can make this more of a cigar mauler than a cigar cutter. Think of a Sears-Roebuck log-splitter. And though the blades may start out sharp, they won't stay that way forever, and the way the force is applied make this kind worse with duller blades than the other two above. Plus the size of the wedge is not adjustable and on all but the smaller rings, can leave large portions of filler "uncapped," impeding draw, since a cigar is not designed to allow smoke to pass transversely across the filler. Bigger rings may not even fit into a given V cutter, no matter how hard you shove.

Some guys love the V, but I say leave it. Far better, I think, is a clean slice across the crown, exposing most of the filler, but leaving a small circle of cap left to hold the wrapper together.

The Punch

With these, you simply punch, or "drill," a hole through the cap and into the cigar, with the bore fixed and determined by the size of the punch. These are the worst, since very little filler is actually exposed and too much leaf is left hanging around near the path of the smoke, which has a tendency to accumulate condensing "tar" (actually contaminant-laden water) and let it drip unceremoniously, and rather unpleasantly, into your mouth.

If you go this route, there are all sorts of cleverly fashioned punches on the market, most of which are hollow, with a circular blade (imagine the horror of sharpening that!) on the end. If you are a cheap and handy fellow, I would think that an 8-penny nail is just about right. I would avoid galvanized nails.

Teeth

Not pretty to watch, especially when bits of leaf remain in the teeth, but a very popular and by far the most practical method. A few pointers, for those ready to take the plunge. First, don't try and bite the end off the cigar. Wrapper tobacco is delicate and must be approached much like a woman.

Begin by gently nibbling and tugging on the cap, a bit out from the center. Whisper as the cap begins to yield. The point is to soften and carefully tear, since most of our teeth, even those of the most carnivorous among us, cut with something less than the precision of sharpened steel. So softly bite and tug at the same time and a section of cap will slide off, leaving a not quite perfect hole, but big enough for good draw, and with enough cap remaining to hold things together. For the piece in your mouth, follow whatever rules you use for chewing gum, olive pits, or spent toothpicks.

Myself, I like to keep my boyhood spitting skills sharpened with them, greatly enhancing my image amongst the non-smoking set. For the more refined, consider a spoon, as you would for a bit of stone found in your lentil soup.

Just a bit of practice and a few ruined, cheap, cigars, will give you this skill, and then you're off to amaze your friends.

We Have Ignition!: Lighting Do's and Don'ts, Or Flaming With Style

Proper technique requires two things: the right fire and the right application. Fire first.

The Right Flame

You must require a flame burning at precisely 340 degrees Fahrenheit. Any more, and you risk carbonizing the tobacco. Any less, and you get incomplete ignition, and your cigar will knock.

Just kidding, of course, but everyone says butane or a quality wooden match only. Or a bit of smoldering firewood, if you have it handy and are in the mood. Paper matches and lighter-fluid, Zippo-type lighters are no-no's, for the same reason: they produce a flame with nasty-tasting residues which will spoil the taste of a cigar. Paper matches have chemicals in them to help them burn, and lighter fuel is kinda like kerosene. Butane burns clean and whatever flavor wood may impart appears not to be objectionable.

As a practical matter, the smoke from a cigar is slightly more substantial a thing than is, say, the fragrance of a rose, and any flavor lent by the bad flames is likely to go unnoticed unless the flame is applied for a peculiarly long time. I avoid paper matches when I can, but notice no real difference when I must use them. I can not remember the last time I used a Zippo - or a burning bolt of magnesium, for that matter - so if these nostalgic lighters appeal to you, you must fire up and judge for yourself.

Car lighters, electric and gas stoves, and gas barbecues are all pretty much OK. Avoid charcoal which has been soaked in starting fluid, and burning buildings and vehicles, since these last may contain mixed fuels of unknown type.

Torching It Off, Or Proper Application of the Flame

Here, I pretty much concede the party line. Apply the flame just below the bottom tip of the cigar and slowly rotate the cigar so that it lights evenly, gently puffing the whole while. Remember that cigar tobacco is moist and that it will not instantly flare up like cigarette tobacco, which actually has agents added to enhance the burn rate. So give it time, keep rotating, until the end glows nice and red all around. Just a moment is all it takes, but you want to do more than merely blacken the tobacco. It must burn. All the way around. Don't worry if the flame actually touches (gads!) the tip of the cigar, so long as no C.A. writers are around. Better too close than too far away.

The party elite suggest you first hold the cigar out of your mouth and gently toast the end, with the flame an inch or so away form the tip, before lighting as above. This looks very impressive as you lounge in your tux or smoking jacket, but I think makes no difference in the smoke.

If you actually want to spend more time lighting than smoking, try using the sun-and-magnifying-glass method. Stand out of the shade, with cigar in mouth, and hold the glass above so as to focus the light on the tip of the cigar. This is likely to take some time, to get all the angles right. Sometimes it is helpful to have an assistant look at the cigar tip for you and report, since you will not be actually able to see it yourself. Do not look into the glass! On a summer's day in the tropics, you should be smoking by margarita time. In winter, you should be able to prolong the pleasure of lighting until the tulips start to sprout.

Band Management

A great debate rages and smolders over whether it is better to smoke with the band on, or to remove it.

The only really important issue is this one: the band is glued on - and not with the special, mysterious-but-benign goo, either - and most often a bit of glue seeps out and makes the band stick to the wrapper of the cigar. Removing it means risking tearing the wrapper in the process, "blowing the seal," and causing your cigar to become leaky and disfigured. You can fix it with a technique in the repairs section, but why spend more time in the shop than you have to? If you must remove the band - and far better to remove it than to smoke it, for you die-hards who smoke every inch - at least wait until the cigar's been burning for awhile, and has had a chance to warm up. This usually softens the glue and allows easy removal. Try and take the band off the opposite of the way it went on, by pulling at the tab left folded over. Sometimes, this remains tight, even though the band is loose from the cigar (you can tell this if the band will rotate - but don't try too hard if it will not), and you must tear the band along the axis of the stogie. This is an advanced technique and fraught with risk.

Leaving the band on announces to the company you at the moment keep what a fine, power-smoke you hold in your hand, or just what a cheap bastard you really are. Assuming, of course, that your company knows the difference. It can be a great conversation-starter among like-minded folk. Personally, when I think about it at all, I do this: With an expensive cigar, I will remove the band, because that's the unassuming, unpretentious kinda guy I am. I wish to intimidate no one with my super premiums! Since most of the time I am smoking an unbanded bundle cigar, this is not an issue. If someone asks, I tell them that I'm an unassuming, unpretentious kinda guy, and I wish to intimidate no one with my super premiums. Then, in my best conspiratorial whisper, first swearing them to secrecy, I tell them it's one of my thousands of Cuban Cohibas, blessed by Raul Castro, and flown up from Miami in the dark of moonless night, before walking nonchalantly away, mumbling something about being late for a meeting with "the ambassador."

Really, I think, the band thing is a non-issue. Do what pleases you most. Just don't tear the wrapper.

The Refined Art of Civilized Puffing

This one really needs little description and I will not resort to base and tasteless analogies. You create slight vacuum in your mouth and the smoke pours out. Mouth only, no lung! Puffing too fast, and the cigar will burn too fast and hot. Slow down, and it will fly right. Too slow, and it will go out! This creates an unhappy state of affairs, as you'll see in a moment. Cigars must be constantly puffed, or they <u>will</u> go out. In as little as 3 minutes or so. The leaf begins moist, becomes more so as it is smoked, and is not soaked in diesel fuel like cigarettes to offset this. Light no cigar you do not intend to smoke. Love your cigar, pay attention to it! Or, like a lover, it will turn cold, hard, and brittle on you. And be nowhere as sweet when you finally manage to bring it around again.

Relighting An Ignored Cigar, And Other Sad Tales

As we have seen, an unpuffed cigar will go out on its own. When relit, it will taste stronger and nasty, mostly because the "tar" has had a chance to condense, congeal, and saturate the remaining filler. The degree of nastiness increases with the length of time the cigar stays out. This is an iron law of cigar smoking and you must not try to break it. The sentence is harsh.

Lately tubes - insert the cigar, screw the cap tight - have been offered which purport to put a cigar out so quickly and painlessly that they smoke like new when removed from the sarcophagus, hours, days, or millennia later. I even have a doctor client-friend who swears by his double-barreled model (to kill two cigars at once?) and says they taste as good when exhumed, but he also tells me he "can smell death" without examination when a patient is near the end, so I wonder. But I am careful to be sniffed by him on a regular basis, just in case, so that I may keep my will current.

I do not believe that any such technique can work. Once out, the cigar cools, and the smoke within it settles out and changes it. Like death, the process is irreversible at our current level of knowledge, though the future holds great promise. When finally solved, the technology will surely be far more sophisticated than a primitive tube. I, in fact, am at this moment conducting brave experiments, cutting off the burning heads of cigars, ignoring their shrieking protests, and quickly sucking the still-hot smoke out with a modified Kirby vacuum cleaner (which the salesman assured me could save cigars), before laying them out on a bed of dry ice. Soon we will transplant Nicaraguan heads onto Canary Island bodies, and then the fools will see! Excuse me, the awaited lightening has finally begun and Igor is calling.

A Cigar's Life Span, Ashing, And The Kind Act Of Extinguishment

Sooner or later, you must pull the plug. Smoke a cigar long enough and even you will smell its death. At some point, either you run out of time, or the cigar begins to taste "sour," as smoke byproducts are filtered out by the remaining filler, and alter taste as they are again consumed in the fire.

How Long To Smoke

For most folks, this occurs about two-thirds the way down the cigar.

I generally continue longer, to where about an inch or so is left. But remember that I am a fiend and that your tastes may be quite different.

The point will also vary with the quality and make-up of the cigar, and how you are feeling that particular day. Some cigars are so delightful that I smoke until my fingertips burn, and then mourn the loss. Others taste horrible and I throw them away after a few puffs. Whatever the point, you will know when it has arrived.

Proper Ashing Technique

On ashing, tradition has held that it is best to leave the ash until it falls off by itself, and that the long ash acted as a radiator, helping to control the fire and cool the smoke. In fact, one measure of a cigar's quality was how long an ash it would hold before it finally fell off. What monster ashes I beheld in the old days! Seems like ages since I've said, "What a nice ash!"

Modern thought - and especially in the interest of overall tidiness - maintains that the cigar should be ashed on a regular basis, that long ash produces little if any benefit. And I agree. More importantly, it is impolite to keep an undisciplined cigar, allowed to ash whenever and wherever it chooses. Curb your cigar and be sure the ashes go in the ashtray, or on the ground outdoors, instead of on your lapel, or in your lady's lap.

Well-made cigars, of course, will have long potential ashes, because of the long filler and symmetrical construction like entubar or accordion. But don't let them have their way with you.

Putting It Out And Disposing Of The Corpse

When the time to lay the beast to rest finally comes, the best course is to do just that: lay it down and let it go out. Shortly it will fade into it own goodnight and can be disposed of when cool, though I always like to be sure, and run water over them before tossing in the trash, or simply flush them in the toilet. Know that a cigar left in the commode unflushed for any period makes not a pretty sight, looking like, well, you know, and leaching out great stains of brown water.

Just let it go out, unattended in the ash tray. Only takes a moment or so. Any attempt to rush this without water by the impatient - like trying to snuff it out like a cigarette - will only make a great mess of things. Sparks go everywhere, the size of the cigar mushrooms as its construction is ruined, and the fire actually flares as more surface area of filler is exposed to oxygen, venting great gouts of smoke. Do this and it will take longer to finally die. It will spite you, curse you, and die badly, causing murmurs of cruelty from those around you. Plus it will fill the entire ashtray and instead of lying in dignified state, will require a closed coffin.

Outdoors, it is perfectly acceptable, and awfully green and politically correct, though Greenpeace might never see it that way - to simply toss the cigar on the ground, provided you are sure it is out and can't start a fire. It will decompose nicely without help, thank you, being composed entirely of untreated leaves. Ever heard the greenies grouse about the oak leaves on your lawn? The same thing, really. For those who find big butts a bit unsightly - and they may linger for awhile, especially without rain - use the shredding technique favored by my Dad: tear the cigar up - just a rip from top to bottom will do - give a shake and toss the liberated leaf bits to the wind. This will give just as much information as a true dissection and can be lots more fun.

Or adopt my more brutal practice of simply grinding them under sole or heel, until rendered nothing more than an unrecognizable pile of brown bio-mass, which scatters quickly.

Smoking Etiquette

While on that brutal note, remember that many nonsmokers view us that way. Worse still than perpetuating that image, a lack of consideration of others is impolite. Launching great clouds of smoke in a confined area, especially where it is not clearly acceptable, is simply not a civilized thing to do.

So don't do it.

Life is too short to spread ill-will for such a trifling reason and if you choose to smoke, you have no right to force your exhaust on others.

Do not become neurotic abut this. Feel free to laugh at those who complain if you smoke outdoors, but be good enough to stand downwind of them.

So here are a few guidelines. Before lighting up anywhere you are not absolutely sure cigars are welcomed, ask. Be sure to be in a smoking section. Ask the waiter or bartender, or the bowling alley keeper, if cigars are O.K., since they do emit a good deal more smoke than cigarettes. After gaining permission, signal your intentions by waving the unlit beast around, and see if you catch a rise. You will be extra polite if you ask those around you if anyone minds. Then feel free to fire up. If someone then complains and if you feel it is justified - like smoke makes them sick, but then why are they in the smoking section? - and you are very nice person, put it out or go outside into the rain. Or not, as the situation warrants. If such a complaint is made by a cigarette smoker, feel free to laugh, or to agree if they also promise not to smoke. Make light of it and make friends. Most such complaints actually stem from unrelated frustrations of the complainer, and have little to do with the smoke. Some believe that such a complaint is simply the right thing to do, and they know not why. So make some joke (not about them!) and break the tension. If the concern seems to be genuine and the smoke actually causes real discomfort, you will of course want to put the baby out. Won't you? There's a good fellow. There's plenty more in the bundle, when you go home.

No, no, no! Don't tell them their hair makes you sick, could they please bleach it back? Be nice. Forget it. It's only a cigar, after all.

CHAPTER EIGHT

Cigar Repairs You Can Make In Your Bathroom

Don't think we will work miracles here. If you get to this point, the prognosis is usually poor. There is a chance we can save the poor thing, but the odds are against him.

Tools

These are pretty basic, as the art is still in the witch-doctor phase. In fact, as far as I know, I am the only fellow foolish enough to ever try and codify cigar repair. Realize that I made must of this stuff up, er, invented it - though I do practice it when called for - and be kind.

Here they are. First, you will want a guillotine cutter, or a very sharp knife, on hand. Also, some sort of probe, long and very thin, preferably with a cutting edge. I use a stiletto I got at an auction once, cleverly hidden in the stem of a very long pipe which was plumbed to actually work! By the time I got it, all that was left was the knife and its pipe-stem sheath. As a guide, my "probe" is about a foot long, with a double edged blade about a ¼ inch across and very thin. Possibly a knitting needle would do, or an old hat pin. Or something you can fashion out of scrap steel, and so finally put to use the Craftsman bench grinder you got for Christmas in 1986, which is probably still in the box. Finally, you will want old cigar parts, mostly wrappers. Do <u>not</u> use pieces from smoked cigars - except bits of wrappers for small patches, they smell too bad! Rather save whole cigars that are obviously beyond repair when you pull them from the cellophane - like hopelessly overfilled ones. These "donors" I keep in an empty box in my humidor.

Before we begin, have a stiff belt of the spirit of your choice. This can get messy. In order of increasing hope for recovery, here is my butchery.

The Plugged Cigar

The term is used to describe a cigar that draws poorly, or not at all. There are two possible causes. A true plug, where leaf lies perpendicular to the axis of the cigar, and blocks the passages. And simple overfilling, where so much filler was used in the bunch that the mold compressed it down to the consistency of a brick, and the passages have been squashed shut.

Before you get scrubbed and ready to operate, be sure that you ain't dealing with a faux plug, a cigar that won't draw because you didn't clip it right. Like because you gave it a tentative little nip with your teeth, or poked a 1/16" hole with a straightened paper clip, and pronounced it kosher. You must remove enough cap to expose nearly all the filler, or you cut down on the draw, and encourage the accumulation of nasty juice near your mouth. Which, again, is why the guillotine is best.

The first thing to know is that the plugged area is usually only at one point in the cigar, and that if you can find and deal with it, you may save it. There is little hope for a uniformly overfilled cigar and it should have a fine future as an organ donor. But most overfilled cigars are merely so in spots and hence savable.

Begin by probing the cigar, taking care to begin at the center of the cap area, and keep the probe parallel as you run it through, so as not to skewer the wrapper from the inside. It is important to use a very thin implement, since an overfilled cigar - especially - can not stand much more volume within it and not burst. If bursted, it's busted. To the parts box, Igor. The object here is to pierce the plug, if a real one is in there. Carefully withdraw the probe and see if draw has improved. If so, good! With even greater care, run the probe through at different points, getting closer to the wrapper now, but still parallel to it at all points. You want to put as many holes in the plug as possible. Good luck!

If this fails, you're probably dealing with an overfilled situation. The next step is to insert the probe in the center hole again, all the way, and slowly and carefully rotate the probe, as if you were boring or coring the cigar. You want to create a passage where none apparently exist. You want to enhance separation between the filler leaves more than actually drill a hole, so don't overdo it. If you actually make a hole, it will always eventually penetrate the burning head as you try to smoke, and instead of drawing smoke, will only suck air from one end of the cigar to the other, even if you manage to get it lit. Which is to say you will draw more air than smoke, having made an un-repairable leak. And once cored and lit, she ain't even good for parts.

If this still doesn't work, get out the guillotine. Not to ready an execution, but we are getting close. Try and feel along the cigar, to spot the tight points. Make your best guess and cut off the tight part from the end which leaves you the longest segment to smoke. Shove the cigar all the way into the cutter and cut it in two! If lucky, you will be left with a good sized and well-drawing segment. Worst case gets you lots of frustrating little pieces. But you may feel better.

If you are so fortunate as to wind up with a "good" hunk, remember that the wrapper has been liberated from its confines, at least at one end of whatever is left, and that it will unravel if you don't wet if and "comb" it back into place. Water - or saliva - is not glue, but will hold long enough. Or you may wrap a big patch - details in a page or two - around the unfettered end.

The Uneven Burn

These come from book construction or uneven fill, where one side of the cigar at that point has more filler than the other. Besides being unsightly, such a burn really degrades the quality of the smoke, making it taste half-dead, almost as if it had been put out and relit. Which makes sense, since part of it is out, or nearly so. You have better chances with the uneven fill, but try the following whatever the reason seems to be. Can't hurt.

Technique one is fright by fire. Tell the cigar that you must burn it for its own good and if that doesn't set it right, you will cut it. Apply lighter to the side which is lagging, puff profusely, and try to burn it into alignment again. Very often this will work, at least for awhile, and it can be used repeatedly to reign in a delinquent cigar.

If the lighter doesn't help, Plan B is to cut off the head with the guillotine, and light again. Do this very quickly, before the smoke has a chance to cool within the cigar. Slide the guillotine over from the wet end, not the burning head! At the very least this will give you many minutes of proper burn, before she goes bad again - if she ever does. Good luck!

The Leaky Wrapper

With this one, we get an almost 100% recovery rate. The problem here is where the wrapper has been somehow compromised and air leaks in when you draw. The wrapper may have been bruised and torn when you pulled the cigar out of the cello, you animal. It may be an imperfect leaf that was not patched at the factory. You may have torn it when you removed the band. However the wrapper became perforated - even if so after you've lit the cigar - you can fix it, fast and easy. For this one, you really do need to go to the bathroom, because you need water to work the magic. Here goes.

First, you need to locate the tears or holes in the wrapper. Next, fabricate a patch from a donor in your morgue box, preferably using donor wrapper. Harvest your donors this way: try and "unwind" the donor's wrapper, and, if she won't unwind (and often she won't), sharply slice down the entire length of the donor cigar, like you did on the frog's abdomen back in Junior High. Carefully remove the wrapper and then the binder, which may require another slice. Wrapper is best for patches, but binder will work in a pinch, like when you are out of wrapper and no cigars have been found on the roadside lately. Discard the filler, or save it for your pipe. We've all tried that <u>once</u>. While you are there, have a look at it to see how it is made, and what is inside. Make the donor's sacrifice count for something.

Anyway, to fabricate a patch, get a piece of wrapper that looks about big enough to cover the holes with a good margin on all sides, and then thoroughly but gently soak the delicate wrapper patch in water. When wet and limp, wrap the patch around the hole like you would a Band-Aid around your finger, with about the same tension. Give just a minute to dry, then light up. The warmth from the smoke will complete the drying and give good adhesion, and on your merry way you go. And the best thing about such a patch, is that you can smoke right through it. Just don't think that this new surgical skill gives you some kind of "I'm a healer!" right to blow Wednesdays off to play golf. 'Cause it don't.

When Worms Strike

Bill's Tale Of The Mouse In The Cigar.

When just out of college as a disenchanted chemist, I began my "professional" career as a "door knocker" for a solar energy company. I would go through neighborhoods, find good applications for the equipment my company sold, and generate leads for the salesmen by enchanting with my youthful charm those folks who lived in the houses my compass told me could use the systems. One of the salesmen was a great tall fellow named Bill Yeager, and, seeing me smoking cigars at the tender age of 22 or so, told me this story:

It seems a cigar smoking acquaintance of Bill's had trouble with the draw and taste of one of his smokes and, ripping the stick apart, was appalled to find a dead, decayed, and half-smoldering mouse inside. His reaction and revulsion was so profound that, Bill told me, the fellow went blind on the spot with the horror of it all. Similar to a story that my father told me about a bit of meat he had found in a bad bottle of Pepsi, back in old Brooklyn when pizza pies cost a quarter, and any sort of cola would remove the paint from a car. Turned out to be bad paint, by the way, not bad cola. I do not know if Bill was serious or not, but the story does well set the stage for the true horror of the cigar world, the **worms** (at this place imagine sharp strikes of bow on violin string). Except that after that tale, what follows don't seem so bad, after all.

It seems that there is a particular sort of worm - a beetle larvae, actually - that loves to eat tobacco leaves during its formative weeks. If I thought you cared about the beasties' name, I'd tell you, 'cause I just looked it up, but I know you don't. I truly haven't seen any of these in at least five years, undoubtedly because of better control by the farmers and factories. So not to worry, but be en guard, at least a little bit. The evidence of these things is that they bore very clean, precise holes through the sides of cigars. Laser clean, not easily mistaken for simple tears or perforations. Often, if the cigars are undisturbed since the escape, you will see a small amount of "tobacco dust" around the hole, just as if you had drilled a 2x4 with your Black and Decker. If you see such things - and you probably won't - you must know two things. First (don't tell!) I have smoked such host cigars, and have lived to tell, have not lost my eyesight, in fact, could tell no difference. I didn't know enough back then to patch the leak, so I just put my finger over the hole. Second, if you care, you must quarantine all the cigars in that particular humidor (or just the box or bundle if not in a humidor, or otherwise within easy "jumping distance" of the discovered lair) and thoroughly inspect the empty humidor for insects. Leaving it open for a week would not be a bad idea.

What to do with the bad cigars is up to you. I think that I would segregate them into different quarantine batches and toss those where I spotted further activity.

R. Hacker, in his <u>The Ultimate Cigar Book</u>, (Autumngold, 1993, 1996) suggests the "cure"...a two day sojourn for the zip-lock-sealed cigars in the freezer. This will kill the worm, yet leave its remains in the cigar, which, to me, is little different from smoking the unfrozen, still-slithering critters. And the temperature and humidity conditions in a freezer, or refrigerator, for that matter, are so cigar-adverse that I think you might as well have thrown them away in the first place. Even with a bag, the cold air gets very dry and, even if you avoid ice crystals in the cigars and they survive, they must be nursed back to proper humidity very slowly and carefully. A dry cigar - from whatever cause - exposed too quickly to moist air will "bloat" and split it's wrapper quicker than a donut maker can let out his pants. Let dry cigars sit in moderately humid conditions before sending them to the humidor and hope for the best. Like in a bathroom, but not after showers. And know that a re-humidified cigar will never completely recover its former glory.

So you are unlikely to ever see this scourge of cigars. But if you do, and are of crude bent, isolate and smoke. If not, toss the holed ones and learn. Or pull a Mr. Freeze, convince yourself that you are not so crude and pray.

Congratulations, cigar-surgeon, on the occasion of your graduation! Keep practicing, continue to cut well, and remember, spare the knife, and cut back on your lifestyle! I mean spare the knife and lose the cigar!

Now that you know how to carve 'em, lets talk about keeping them healthy in the first place.

CHAPTER NINE

Perfect Storage, And Big, Wonderful Humidors You Can Buy For A Song

Like humans, cigars can only exist within a limited range of conditions. Temperature, air composition, gravity, and an absence of hard radiation all are important to survival. Also, like humans, a narrower range of conditions are required if we want them to thrive. Fortunately, we need not get into any profound exercise and anti-oxidant regimes here. There are really only two important parameters: temperature and humidity. Especially try not, unlike that shop in Tallahassee, to use a transparent humidor exposed to full sun.

The Ideal Conditions For Robust Health

The magic numbers, easy to remember, are 70 degrees and 70% humidity. These may vary a bit, say +/-10 either way, but the 70/70 rule is good and easy to remember. Humidity is the primary criterion, but since it varies with temperature, both are important. To maintain these conditions, you need two things: a container that can be sealed - called a humidor - and a device to measure temperature and humidity.

This is important! A cigar too dry will smoke hot, harsh, dull, and fast. Too wet, and not only will it be hard to light - and keep lit - but you run the risk of mold growth, and of having the wrapper split open as the filler absorbs too much water, and expands. Note that any quick change in conditions - like removing a cigar from your warm, humid overcoat pocket to light it in the frigid Chicago winter air - can instantly promote damage, like a split wrapper. Like aquarium fish floating in their plastic bags, cigars should be acclimated slowly when conditions change. And especially, when you travel by air, pack your cigars in your carry-on bags. The freezing (even in July, it's cold up there) environment found in many airline cargo holds can ruin them. If you must check them, make sure they wind up in the pet section. And if they come back smelling of cat urine, well, you knew better.

Devices To Monitor The Ideal Conditions

For a long time, this was a dicey proposition at best. Getting a good thermometer was no trick, but the mechanical humidity gauges offered for cigar storage, regardless of price, were notoriously inaccurate. They are still offered and often come installed in humidors sold for home or office use. And they are pretty things, lending a nostalgic old-tech look to the box. But I suggest against buying them, or relying on them if you get one with the box you buy.

Far better are the digital devices now available, most apparently made in the same factory in China. The first one I bought is branded an Airguide, got through a company I saw mentioned in C.A. It cost $50 or so, but I have since seen the same unit at Radio Shack - no great discounter itself -for about $22. They give a constant LCD readout of temp and relative humidity, and can be accessed to give the min/max range of readings since the unit was last reset. This last feature can be useful if you like to collect data, but as far as I am concerned, yesterday is a canceled check, and are my cigars still fresh today? The little units are accurate, cheap, and highly recommended. You should run out to Radio Shack now and get one. I'll wait for you to get back before I continue.

How To Maintain The Ideal Conditions

Temperature is pretty much subject to that prevailing in your home or office, so have a good heart-to-heart with your thermostat - and your family - from time to time. The mostly-closed box of your humidor will change temperature more slowly than the air in your house, what with open doors and all, but it will change. Fortunately, cigars like it just about the same as humans do. Anyway between 60 and 80 degrees is "cool."

Humidity is a bit more of a problem. Even as I sit here in Florida, the most humid state, in June, one of the most humid months, the humidity meter on my desk only reads 58%. (I don't keep it on my desk; I got it out so I could tell you about it). Without the AC, it would be higher, in the 90's, just like outside. So in the house it gets to be too high in temperate months, like October, because the heat/AC is off. Anyway, you get my point: most of the time, conditioned household air is too dry. You need to introduce some water vapor into the confined space of your humidor. If your house air occasionally gets too humid, leave the humidor open and run a dehumidifier, like I do.

An important point is to <u>always</u> use distilled water in your humidifying agent. Always. At a buck a gallon, you get a multi-year supply.

While I do not speak from personal experience, everyone in the cigar world says that tap water (and mineral water, I guess, too) can promote mold and foul flavor. I don't know why this may be so, but at a buck a gallon, there seems no good reason to find out.

My humidifying agent, for my large humidor, is quick, dirty, very effective and very cheap, which is O.K. because no one ever sees it. I took a largish kitchen-style sponge, and found a Tupperware-type container about the same size, in all dimensions. I cut large vents into the container's top with a razor knife. The sponge sits inside, soaked in distilled water. When the humidor seems to be too moist, I put an empty cigar box on top of it, sliding it back and forth across the vents, since the amount of exposed surface area regulates the evaporation rate, and hence the humidity. You see, Dr. Sheets, I do remember something from Physical Chemistry! You can cover it up completely if conditions get too wet, but this has not been a problem. Besides, cigars adjust in their humidity slowly, over a period of days or longer, so you have plenty of time to correct before things get drenched. This is my solution. For smaller humidors, I used to take a bit of sponge and stick it into an old 35mm film container, which I had pin-cushioned with holes. You get the idea. Experiment. But have a care to not over-soak a sponge unless there is a leak-proof tray, sans holes, beneath it, like my Tupperware container, above. Use a new sponge, not one saturated with ammonia and Comet, and used by your wife in the bathroom, and God knows what on.

Commercial devices are available in the shops and catalogs to serve the same purpose, but many do not work well, and have such limited water capacity that they require frequent attention, without which the cigars may go to dust. One of the many hidden beauties of my sponge method is that it will go months at a time without recharge.

Of the commercial systems, those made by Credo are generally considered to be the best. They are said to work as humidistatic devices, maintaining constant humidity so long as properly charged with water. In these days of super cigar popularity, I am sure there are a rash of competitors, many of which will work well. But the principle will always be the same: a holder for a material which will "suspend" water, and allow it to evaporate at a controlled rate. Like a sponge in a Tupperware container, or traveling soap dish.

Temporary Storage And Old Man Winter

Cigars will keep reasonably well for days and even weeks at a time outside a conditioned environment, the time depending on just how hot and dry it is where you happen to be. July in Germany gives longer life than July in hot steamy Florida, which still is better than dry, frying Arizona. The heated, or air conditioned hotel or office is better than the car in the parking lot. A good rule of thumb is that if the place is comfortable enough for you to sleep in, the cigars will be O.K. for awhile. They can be kept in their box or bundle. If concerned, add a bit of moistened tissue, wrapped in tin foil or such. You have more important things to worry about than your cigars, anyway.

For extended stays, some sort of traveling humidor is a must, since even the better cigar boxes leak like the proverbial sieve. Anything reasonably air tight will do, like a jumbo zip-lock bag, a larger Tupperware container, like that. Remember to use some sort of humidifying agent, like the film containers we talked about, or some wet toilet paper stuffed in an empty tunafish can, or loosely wrapped in a baggie. If you must use tissue, be sure to wet it frequently, as it is not a high capacity storage medium. A bit of sponge will last longer. Do use water, not cologne or shampoo. It don't need to be distilled for the short term, for cigars whose time is nearly up.

Of course, feel free to spend a small fortune on any of the lovely "traveling humidors" to be found on the market. They do look neat and make wonderful gifts for the smoker who has everything, but strike me as about as useful as those traveling bar kits - complete with measuring cups and martini shakers - that I used to see at the auctions.

For packing cigars for the day, I usually just shove a few in my pocket and leave them in my briefcase, or to swelter in my car under the Florida sun. Don't hurt 'em much, for the day. You can buy all kinds of cigar holders, from leather cigar "fingers" to wooden and metal tubes and boxes, and, believe me, I have my share in the collection. Up in my closet some where, I think. Great gift ideas and nice additions to your "equipment." But I haven't used one in years, since I usually have pockets with me. Though I used to thoroughly enjoy the ritual of packing my 'five-shooter" leather cigar holder, carefully putting it in just its place in my ultra-thin briefcase, before racing off to the office, and the wonder of which stocks had moved, and which clients would be pleased. Of course, I could smoke in the office back then, which no doubt added to the anticipation, and the joy of preparation.

That winter bit can be tough, though. Winter air is so cold that the moisture content (relative to 70 degrees) is non-existent, and cigars can go from warm-and-happy-under-the-armpit to bone-dry-freezing in a minute or two. This can cause the cigar to split it's wrapper as the outside dries much faster than the still-moist and protected inside. Coddling can help, but most of you won't take the time to keep the stogie under your hat for a few blocks, or to blow moist breath on it for awhile inside one of your gloves. Or to tuck it under your scarf. Me, when I am (now, thank goodness, very rarely) subjected to such conditions, take my chances and light 'em up. And toss the beasties that don't obey.

On Age And Aging

Cigars improve with age. No doubt about it. A green cigar, just popped out of the mold, will smoke hot, harsh, and thoroughly vile. Even the best Cuban. Given a month or so, it will mellow and improve. Several months, it will mature and increase in depth and complexity. A year or two - if, like a great wine, it had the right stuff to begin with - and it will approach the stuff divine. The upper end for most cigars, I think, is several years at best, though there have been reports of mid-twentieth-century Cubans becoming great after all those years. Or still being good, or being but a shadow of their former selves, but still good. Who can judge? Even if someone smoked the exact same cigar 40 years ago, the memory is sure to be much less than perfect. And oh, the price if you can find them!

The important points about aging are these. If you get cigars that smoke bad and seem too young, lay them down (like the Grateful Dead song) for a few months, and see. If you get cigars that you think are exceptional, lay them down, noting date, and see. You'll probably get as much of a charge from the "time capsule" feeling as from any improved taste. You outer child, you. For the truly anal, carefully record date, flavor and impressions, smoking environment, and how you feel. Smoke one at least at one-month intervals, collecting all data, especially how you feel. Not just about the cigar, but about all things at the time. Be sure to use moisture-resistant paper and store the notes in your humidor. Human consciousness being as subjective as it is, your records won't have much value, but you will <u>feel</u> much better. For a little while, anyway.

So aging is essential, to begin the cigar's life with. The stouter improve longer. And you may play with aging on your own, if it pleases you. Lay them down, pull one every couple of months, record your impression, like that.

But mostly I just smoke the cigars in my humidor, unless I get some young ones, or overly dry or wet ones. And, yes, cigars that seem to be too moist should be brought gradually 'round, in the humidor, just like those guppies. The same goes for any dried out ones you find under the seats of your car, that you want to resurrect.

The Inevitability Of Marriage

Cigars are aromatic things. Which means they smell, they are volatile, they give off odors from the oils which make the tobacco taste so good. Once a neglected cigar has had most of it's oil "boil off," it is dead. Evermore. In fact, one of the important reasons behind humid storage is to keep these oils at bay, from evaporating at too rapid a rate, and robbing the cigar of that which makes it so flavorful. Oil and water and all that. But even within the confines of your humidor, these vapors will travel. And light on other cigars, to be absorbed, for a time, by them. The short of it is that cigars stored in the same humidor will in this way exchange their flavors, in a great airborne orgy of vapor-pressure pollination. They will grow to taste more like each other. Not entirely, especially different types, but they will exchange flavor. This process is referred to in the trade as "marrying" and, in the preliminary aging in the factory, is one of the ways that brand consistency is maintained. How you feel about such relations after the fact is up to you. If prudent, er conservative, I mean, if you want to discourage this sort of thing, then physical barriers, like wooden separators in your humidor, or using the original boxes, are said to retard the process. Cigars laid wrapper to wrapper, without even the "protection" of the cellophane wrapper (and you know what that looks like, after the cigar is removed..), are most at risk.

By the way, the removal of the cello both dramatically enhances the aging, and the courtship. If you want your cigars to grow old alone, remove the cello, and shut them back in their box. Ignore any flowers found on their lids.

The Wide World Of Humidors

Those Finely Crafted Dearly Vended Boxes

They are making some wonderful stuff these days. Gorgeous, hand crafted, incredibly precise humidors. Small and chic, for desk or library table. Generous and breathtaking, to replace your china cabinet. End table and occasional table size. In the shape of pyramids. Covered with exquisite veneer, dyed the colors of the rainbow. Deeply inlaid, in the manner of your company's logo, if you will pay enough.

It truly is a golden age of humidors. And no wonder, the market is ripe. Never before have so many humans, all a-jingle with information-age-dinaro, smoked cigars. Then again, never before have some many humans existed at the same time. The market is huge and it is being serviced.

If you long for one of these lovelies, and most really are superb, be prepared to part with at least several hundred dollars for a small one. Those that are both well made (both in terms of aesthetics and seal) and which can hold a significant amount of cigars - and I mean at least several hundred instead of several dozen - begin at a grand or so, and fly up from there. If smitten, indulge. These are fine artifacts and probably worth the price.

So far, I have resisted the urge, mostly because the small ones are more ornaments than storage devices for the volume of cigars I keep, and because hardly anyone (besides me, and then only for the first few weeks) really notices and appreciates the desk top ornaments that already clutter my office. And the big ones are so far out of line with the next suggestion that I don't even look at their price tags.

Cedar: the Cigar's Friend

Let us begin by telling you that cedar is the cigar's friend. Besides smelling nice, being stored near cedar both enhances a cigar's aroma, and seems to promote the aging process. Or at least compliment it. This is why you will so often see humidors lined in cedar or cedar veneer, and expensive cigars sometimes wrapped in a thin slice of this wood. Cedar is an aromatic wood and it's oil goes well with that of cigars.

An Elegant, Expansive, And Brilliantly Cost Effective Alternative

O.K. **Here is the secret that alone is worth twice the price of the book**. The very best humidors are...ready?

Old cedar chests! The kind that are still being made, and have been cranked out at least since the twenties. In every style, from Chippendale and Queen Anne, to Deco, Colonial, and that surprisingly severe stuff they made in the late 50's. In every fashion, spanning nearly a full century. Made from solid cedar and usually covered in fine veneer or solid mahogany or walnut. Made to seal up tight, to keep that lovely cedar odor in, to protect those fine woolens from moths. I mean tight enough to nearly hold a vacuum. Built close - like a wooden boat's strakes - and square, with effective seals. Lane's was and is a premier maker, as is Cavalier. But almost any make will do, as the standards for sealsman-ship were as good or better than now being applied to humidors.

Just be sure it is a cedar chest, for clothes, and not just some old wooden box made to keep dock lines in.

You can get these in almost any size, from dainty and diminutive, to armoires big enough to keep a wardrobe in. Or a suit of armor. Most come in the traditional chest form, though you can find stand-up cabinet- style units if you look.

And, usually, for a song. At auctions, the Salvation Army, second hand shops. Bright and refinished, or under coats of paint. I got a great one for about $50 and another for less. Even a new one should cost tons less than the 8"x10" boxes you see in the catalogs. And serve you far better and be considered a far better investment by your wife.

Trust me on this one. They work great. And a big humidor is lots better, even if it stays mostly empty. You can store all your other cigar paraphernalia in there. Hang your cutters and scissors and party hats from brass cup hooks you screw in the side. You have room to grow and take advantage of whatever plum deals cross your path. Plus plenty of room for sweaters, at least until you get serious.

Humidors For The Truly Cheap

We've covered the Tupperware ground and a little imagination, and a few parties, will get you any size you want. What you what is a container that will seal good and cost less than $15. Right? Spend a few enchanting moments strolling the housewares section of your local K-Mart.

The next avenue is aquariums. A new one if you are a prude and a well-cleaned one if not. But remember W.C. Field's admonition: "Don't drink the water, fish f— in it." Ten gallons should be more than big enough to start and, if you outgrow it, you can give it you your kids to keep, and finally kill, fish in. Be sure to get a good cover, that seems to seal well. Or cut a piece of glass - or Plexiglas - yourself. Most tanks have an inset lip that will give a good seal with a properly sized cover, though be careful to not remove any filter-tube knock-outs if you buy a cover actually designed with fish in mind. Service the humidifying agent often, or Neptune will have his wrath on you. The seal will be good, but usually not great unless you use a plate glass cover with a brick on each corner. If too cheap to buy even a used one, try cruising the neighborhoods the night before trash day. My kids have brought numerous tanks from crystal-with-angelfish to dead-green-and-I-ain't-cleanin'-it in a matter of weeks - like the time they left the tank heater cranked up while we were off on vacation, and we returned to neon tetra stew - and on the curb is where they wound up.. The tanks, that is, not my children. I still have great aspirations for my children.

Other vessels are only limited by your creativity. Empty five gallon paint buckets. These seal great, but must be cleaned well. Ruffles bags and chip clips. Hefty bags. Think about it! You'll get it under $5, if you try.

CHAPTER TEN

The Rest Of The Toys

O.K. We've already covered a lot of the gear which you must exhaust your discretionary income on, like cutters and humidors and burl walnut carrying cases, and the Cigar-Savor type kill 'em quick and it won't mind and come out tasting just fine tubes. Just in case you still have a few coins rattling round in your jeans, here's more stuff. If your spouse protests the expense and threatens to send you to the Isle of Misfit Toys, threaten yourself to buy a boat, the ultimate cash burning device. B.O.A.T., by the way, according to Don, one of my Bahamas-sailing clients, stands for "Bring Out Another Thousand." Of course, if you have one, you know this already.

If what follows does not sate you, spend a Saturday studying the ads in Cigar Aficionado or SMOKE, and Monday arranging for a personal loan with your banker.

Ashtrays

It goes without saying that these need to be big. Not necessarily designed for cigars, but large. There are many beauties from which to choose, both new and "antique," often in glass but ceramic, brass, bronze, and other metals as well. Table top and floor models. If you want an old one, and have the time, many joyful discoveries await in the auctions and antiques shops. Just remember that a large, substantial ashtray is a blunt object, and could provide a one-way trip to that

Isle, if you push your honey hard enough. Not so pleasant to
have one fall on your foot, either. Many very nice new ones
are being made, but be prepared to spend at least several
hundred if you want a real work of art from a fine crystal
house. Look in the back issues of C.A. - which you can search
on their Web page - for a good article on these and on lots of
other toys. And, by the way, bronze is far more masculine a
material than crystal and, while still a blunt object, is not
subject to shatter if you drop it on your hardwood floor. More
likely, it will dent the oak, or shatter the bones in your foot.
How about a nice Art Nouveau piece, with unclad nymphs
cavorting about the rim, sporting with the cigar you carefully lay between them?

Of the older ones, especially consider the "floor model"
types which blossomed during the 30's and 40's. Basically a
stand designed to hold a large ashtray at about sitting-hand
height, most of these are lovely, interesting pieces of furniture. Brass and alabaster abound in them. Many have match
holders built in. I even have one, in Deco style, with an
illuminated base that looks just fabulous. Again, you need
time to search the shops, auctions, garage and attic sales,
but great buys await, especially compared to what you'd pay
for new stuff.

Of ashtrays designed specifically for cigars, there really
is only one commonly encountered shape, beyond a simple
bowl with extra large (cigar, not cigarette, size) grooves in
the rim. That is the long tray, about the length of a long
cigar with a wide grove for holding, with a receptacle for
ashes at the end. Like the more general types, these come in
many materials and many variations, sometimes with two
or more groves in the tray. My favorite is a varnished teak
one my wife got me for Christmas in '82 or so. The "tray"
part has two grooves -though sadly, the second is almost always empty except when I am burning two cigars at once to
compare them - and is hinged over a compartment which is
too leaky to hold cigars for long, but is just dandy for lighters

and stuff. The receptacle part held a cigarette-sized glass bowl which has long since broken, but the wooden husk in which it sat does just fine.

My least favorite is an East European cast glass colossus, holding one cigar and perhaps three ounces worth of ashes, but being the quintessential blunt object. These last clubs are available in several colors, clear, green, blue, and perhaps several others. None look particularly elegant, but they are inexpensive and are gale-rated paperweights. Leaded glass takes on a whole new meaning...

I have not seen many dedicated cigar ashtrays on the used and antique market, so you will have to look in the catalogs and tobacco shops. Like with humidors, there is a profusion of new product available, to satisfy even the most incorrigible spendthrift. Look around.

Serious smokers will want at least one cigar ashtray near their easy chair and slippers, or wherever they smoke regularly. This is an important accessory. The proper holder really can enhance the smoking experience, or at least not allow the distraction that will come from smoldering stogies constantly vaulting and tumbling out of undersized astrays, onto your wife's prize Persian.

Carpet, that is. If you have a cat, it will permit itself to be so scorched only once, and thereafter be a wary target. I refuse to join the debate over whether it is better to burn cat fur, or fine oriental woven wool. Like I said, the cat will keep moving, anyway, and no one I know is that quick with a cigar. Get a large ashtray and have peace.

Lighters, And Matches to Be Proud Of

With lighters, you must have butane. These can range from the merest Bic, to the grandest Cartier. Plastic or gold, they all pretty much burn the same. There are all kinds available, have been for years, due to the perennial popularity of cigarettes. One word of advice: flint and steel (that rolling wheel you see) is a far more dependable means of ignition than the electric devices the bright boys keep cooking up. Some use batteries, some are peizeo-electric (watch my spelling, Miss Fisher), which just means that some crystals will generate an electric current when you squeeze 'em just right. Just like some women. These high-tech gizmos - and I have had more than my share over the years - have always failed me after a few weeks or months of service. Even the expensive ones. The electrodes get out of alignment, or unclean-ably dirty, or the crystal just won't love you any more. Stick with man's old faithful flint and steel, true friend through the ages. You can get a whole card full of new flints for less than the price of a watch battery.

While on this high-tech note, a recent development has been the "jet flame," where the butane is passed through a venturi and over a catalyst, like platinum wire. This creates a finely tuned flame that looks like rocket exhaust, and will hold up under even the stiffest wind. These are cool. Very cool. The one I bought in Charleston a summer or three ago soon failed me, like all those other painted lighters, but was great fun while it worked. They have gotten cheap enough that some might even consider them disposable, and light just great. Especially in a darkened room, where all your boyhood fantasies of space exploration come quickly back to mind, and to hand.   Whoosh! The fearless Earth pilot, out of ammo, attacks the evil alien mother ship, in desperation using his rocket flame to melt her fuel pods! Success! The mother ship goes up in smoke, in the airless vacuum of space! And home the pilot goes, to adoring women, and unworldly cigars!

If you choose matches, buy wood only. Fireplace matches, hand crafted cigar matches at $2 each. Self striking "Ohio Blue Tip" types if you can still find them, which lend a wonderful rustic air when you smartly pull them alive on the sole of your boot, Cowboy-style. Or the big box, need-a-striker-supermarket-variety if you can not. Just be sure and get wood and keep your wood dry. No matches in the humidor, please!

Jewelry

Gee whiz, you can really knock yourself out here. There's been a small renaissance in cigar-motif jewelry, especially tie tacks, cuff links, shirt studs, and money clips. The best is gorgeous and quite expensive. How about gold cigar cuff links, with platinum ashes and ruby inlaid bands? And matching studs? What a vision at the next smoker night you will make! Or cigar links and flaming match studs? The pages of C.A. and similar magazines are loaded with ads for items like these, and The Cigar Enthusiast - subsidiary of the Wine Enthusiast - at 800.356.8466, has tons of nice cigar toys in addition to cigar jewelry. Not that they are the only ones, but they did mail me a catalog. If you go in for this sort of thing, the Enthusiast has an attractive set in vermeil (gold plate over sterling, a very attractive and durable material) and rubies for about $150 for the set of links and studs. Which is about what a cheap box of their cigars goes for. But get a catalog, it will give a you good idea of what's out there, and some of the accessories' prices seem reasonable. They even, by gosh, have ties, shirts, and - who would have guessed? - cigar socks. If someone complains about the smell of your cigars, offer them your socks? As they say in Jersey and sometimes in New York, <u>forget about it</u>.

The best sign of just how far this madness has gone is offered by the Krieger Watch Corporation (800.441.8433; in FL 305.534.8433), makers of fine Swiss watches and chronometers. For those who don't know what a chronometer is, like I didn't until after I bought my Omega Seamaster - 'cause I liked the three dial look - in Venice, it basically is a watch <u>and</u> a stopwatch that can time up till 12 hours. The side dial - or recorder - is a regular second hand, the top dial gives minutes elapsed, and the bottom dial gives hours elapsed since you punched the button that got the stopwatch second hand going, which is the big one, where you expect the regular second hand to be. The regular second hand is in the side recorder, though, so don't expect the big one to move unless you hit that button! These are great for proving your Bronco really will do 0-60 in under 15 seconds pulling a boat.

Krieger has come out with a series of limited edition watches dedicated to cigars, with a smoking stogie prominent on the dial. The Torpedo, for instance, is a chronometer limited to 100 pieces, which range in price from about $3K to over $16K, depending on materials and style. These are neat watches and include "Pulsometers," which purportedly let you measure your heart rate, from 30 to 200 beats per minute (plenty of room there, what?), so you can see when the nicotine kicks in. Gordon Gekko, are you listening?

So you see, if susceptible you can really get carried away. If these sort of trifles bore you, rest easy, my discussion and mentions of sources ends here. If you are at risk, don't worry, more will follow. Soon, your mailbox will be full of cigar garden tools catalogs, and you will be in credit counseling.

Holders

Said to say, these have really become passé, and probably belong in the collectibles section, although last time I looked they were still being made. Big brother to the cigarette holder, these are just a device to keep the tobacco out of your mouth: a plastic or bone "bit," and a cupped short tube to hold the cigar's head in. I've seen them in amber, wood, ivory, and meerschaum, that lovely, white sea-foam they carve those pretty pipes out of. Actually, meerschaum is a very lightweight mineral, which absorbs tobacco tar as it is smoked through, and turns an ever-deeper lovely brown. They come carved and plain, long and short, and so on. If interested, ask a tobacconist with a good selection of pipes what he can uncover in his wholesale catalogs.

While kinda chic and retro, I think these things detract from the joy of smoking just a bit, keeping you at an antiseptic distance from your cigar, as it were. As Donald, a college buddy, once said in another context, it's like "taking a shower with a raincoat on." And ah, those showers in the "Hotel

Harrington!," er, I mean Harrington Hall. The Eagles' <u>Hotel California</u> had just come out about then. For those who like cigars but detest the wet, moist end, they might be worth a try.

Smoke Filters For The Air

These are probably the one item in the toy store that gets completely unquestioned support from me. Oh, sure, it is nice to be able to light your cigars, and have somewhere besides the floor to ash them. But filters are often overlooked and extremely useful.

The first reason is because smoke of any kind is not good for you, or your wife, or your kids, to inhale. Assuming that your dependents allow you to smoke in your home. Even if just you locked away in a closet, you want to taste the smoke, not breath it.

The second reason is that cigar smoke - or burning leaves or cooking grease, for that matter - will leave a staining, smelly residue where it is allowed to linger. On your hair and cloths, on your walls and windows, in your curtains and upholstery. Left to find it's own home, the smoke will leave an unsightly legacy, an oily, yellowish-brown coating on all it brushes.

Fortunately, in this age of heightened health awareness and bubbleboy-technology, the free market answers. There are units all over the place, in K-Mart and Target, and advertised on the Rush program.

No, they do not have to be special cigar filters. Anything that will pull the particles out of the air will do, thank you. This usually means a big fan and a special paper filter, not unlike those used for automobile air intakes. You want a filter with lots of paper, bundled in lots of baffles. Often it will come with some kind of activated charcoal mesh, whose job it is to remove odors. Which is nice. But the paper pulls the smoke out.

Get one that is sized properly for your regular smoking lair - look on the box for sizing guidelines. Remember to change the filter element once you can't see through it anymore, if you want it to work. And don't be surprised to find that the replacement filter costs half or more what the whole darned thing cost in the first place. Beats opening the windows to the hot, mosquito-laden air, doesn't it?

By the way, while ozone-generators and electrostatic particle filters are nice, remember that your first line of defense against the legacy of the smoke is a big old wad of high-tech paper.

Get one, for you and yours. Don't let it get to the point - as I nearly did - of my doctor friend, whose family got him one for father's day. Beats a tie, I guess, but I would not give up the joy of the new garbage pails I got for father's day for anything. They roll so sweet and save my aging back. They even put ribbons around them and filled them the first time for me, before they woke me up, the darlings. Then again, I guess I did get my wife a Lady Weed Wacker for mother's day a few years back, so it all comes around. And, God bless her, she even used it once or twice. To open packages from Bloomindales and once to chase a stray dog away.

Collectibles

Men, and some women, have been smoking cigars for centuries, now.

Since I promised in the first chapter to not get into the musty details of tobacco history, I must refer you to my upcoming book, <u>War and Cigars: Valiant Stogies Through The Ages, And Into The Millennium</u>. Pay particular attention to the West Indian conspiracy theory, where I nearly prove that Caribbean Islanders promoted tobacco use among Europeans in a diabolical strategy to win back in the 21st century the empire they knew their people would begin losing in the 16th!

Back to the artifacts. Folks have been smoking cigars a long time, and lots of paraphernalia has been manufactured over the decades to tend to their pleasure. Holders. Ashtrays. Matchsafes. Lovely cases in materials from silver and pewter to leather and wood. Advertising items. "Tramp art" covered in cool cigar bands of yesteryear. Grand and unassuming humidors in every wood. Old boxes, in both "dress box" (thin wood - now plywood - boxes covered with colorful paper graphics) and "cabinet box," or all wood, styles. Those magnificent cigar-store Native Americans. Old cutters and trimming tools. Big cigars have for a long time been symbols of affluence, and the big boys of days gone by bought a lot of quality implements to compliment their hobby.

Actually <u>finding</u> this stuff may be a bit difficult. In the days when I was active in the antiques business, I came across very little, probably because cigars were pointedly out of style then, and the dealers didn't pay the stuff much mind when they found it. These days, any dealer with a pulse is looking to cash in on the cigar craze, and will prominently feature - and mark up! - what they do find.

The antiques and collectibles markets are very much one-of-a-kind-gold-is-where-you-find-it kinds, and you really have to look to find the good stuff, both at wholesale and retail. So look. In the shops and shows, at auctions, in flea markets and garage sales. Especially in the last two, if you're seeking bargains from a seller who may not know what they have.

Do a Web search. The stuff is out there, in large quantity, I guarantee it. But it has been subject to the laws of thermodynamics. Entropy has had it's way and you will find it a piece here, in a tin cup in a basement, and a piece there, in the bottom drawer of a pine chest in a shop in Lake Placid. But oh, the joy of discovery when you do make a find!

CHAPTER ELEVEN

Cigar Related Periodicals And Books

Magazines

Cigar Aficionado

Of course, the great granddaddy of them all, the Zeus of the modern cigar age, is <u>Cigar Aficionado</u> (800.992.2442, about $17 for now 6 issues per year), launched by Marvin Shanken 'round about 1993. This magazine is widely credited with sparking the renaissance of high-end smoke by presenting cigars as the truly exquisite treats they are. Targeted to the affluent, the magazine is chock full of articles - and ads - on a wide variety of expensive pastimes, from fine scotches and rums to travel, pens, boats and cars. As well as interviews with celebrities with a cigar smoking bent. The ads are superb and give a look at wonderful things you might not otherwise see. The price is modest (though the ad revenue is not) and the coffee-table look is super. Simply subscribing will probably get you on all types of cigar mailing lists. Highly recommended, even for the casual smoker.

A companion publication is C.A.'s <u>Cigar Insider</u> (800.644.4395; monthly, $60 per year) a newsletter which promises cigar-only, in depth, timely news, with extensive and frequent taste-testings.

Smoke

Another C.A.-class magazine is SMOKE, quarterly at about $17 per year (800.766.2633). I hadn't looked at SMOKE in awhile, seeing it maybe once in the J.R. store on I-95 in North Carolina. It' been around since late '95 or so. I thought I'd better track them down for this section, and I called yesterday to request a sample issue. Andy Marinkovich, Sr. Editor, was kind enough to overnight me one. Boy, am I glad I asked. For you high-end ad junkies, this mag is even thicker with them than C.A.! And while they cover the same sort of related pursuits - travel, gaming, drink, and so forth - as does C.A., SMOKE does it with a bit less reverence, with tongue held more tightly in cheek, a style which appeals to me a great deal and will make you smile. They take themselves less seriously, which makes sense, since we are only talking about cigars here, after all. Take C.A., remove a healthy portion of the Wall Street Journal and Architectural Digest, replace with a dollop of Playboy, and the barest hint of MAD Magazine, and up you go in SMOKE. Recommended without reserve. My favorite.

There are others, but none yet match the importance of these two. You'll find more information on them - and on electronic format magazines - when we tour the Web in the next chapter. Just hold on a little longer.

Cigar Books Worth A Puff Or Two

The several titles that follow are books that try and give a broad overview of the basics of smoking cigars, how to select them, store them, stuff like that. Most of this - and more - you already know from having read this far in the book in your hands. But other, perhaps more reverent, perspectives are always nice, and I've given my opinions on the few that I think are worthwhile. In them, by the way, you agricultural and history buffs will find a lot more on tobacco in field and barn, through the recent ages. Books about cigar related things - stories, collectibles, artwork, and so on - can be found referenced in the next section. The few I review I give you in the order they happen to be laying on my desk:

The Ultimate Cigar Book

Richard Carleton Hacker
Autumngold Publishing, 1993, 1996
You - or at least I - gotta like a guy who says "After all, one of the old adages is, 'The best cigar is the one you get for free.'" Welcome to Richard Hacker, the man who calls himself - and has apparently trademarked - the "Cigar Czar."

Hacker's book is the first one I came across that deals with the cigar mystique as a practical matter, and probably, after my own, my favorite. I found it in a cigar store in Lake Placid, NY, across the street from that antiques shop, and within view of that delightful hotel where the teenagers ran up and down the stairs all night. Richard covers many of the basics well, and though I differ on some areas with him, I can't argue with the purity of his spirit. It's all a matter of personal taste, anyway, which he so honestly points out by rating things by his "HPH," for "Highly Prejudiced HackerScale."

The book is also full of many of the author's own photos of cigar stuff and regions. I, too, am hopeful that my publisher will unleash me with camera on a tour of that Lew Rothman describes as the "Toilets of the Caribbean," and Havana, too! For now, you'll have to check Hacker's book to see them.

I enjoyed his chapters on "Spirits and Smoke," where he gives his views on those beverages which especially compliment cigars - something I'm not qualified to comment on, being "such a sober fellow," in the Roger Rabbit to the private investigator- character sense - and on "Celebrity Cigar Smokers," where you'll find some folks you'd never have imagined to be cigar smokers. Here, in fact, I find that I must correct my George Burns quote on expensive cigars. According to Richard, it goes like this: "If I paid ten dollars for a cigar, first I'd make love to it, then I'd smoke it." Anyway,

The Ultimate Cigar Book is kinda fun, well worth adding to your collection if you can stand to read another book on cigars. And, of course, if you can, we have more.

Nat Sherman's A Passion For Cigars

Joel Sherman and Robert Ivry

Andrews and McMeel, 1996

Another good book, in spite of the fact that theirs is the publisher my agent had wanted to go with my book. "Oh, well, she said, "still plenty others."

These guys also have done a decent job and the book is worth looking at. While a bit shorter and slightly less impassioned than the Hacker book, they do a good job handling the basics, and have outstanding illustrations and graphics. The writing also seems a bit tighter. Especially enjoyable were Joel's reminiscences on his father's days in the cigar business, and on his listing of what his celebrity smoker customers - by name - have preferred in the way of Nat Sherman cigars from his shop. Like Hacker, the Sherman book does give gentle guidance on some of the more prominent brands including excellent coverage of their own... - and will be useful if you want to focus on the higher end stuff in your initial experimentation.

The section on cigar storage is good and they even include a chapter on organizing your own cozy cigar dinners, replete with recipes! Which is where I learned that Joel's dream cigar entree is venison with wine and mushroom sauce, served with creamed spinach and glazed baby carrots. What could top that, but a Nat Sherman Dakota?

The Cigar Companion: A Connoisseur's Guide

A. Bati and S. Chase

Running Press, 1995; foreword by Marv Shanken

This last book is probably the lightest-weight of the three, being primarily occupied with brand listings. I include it here because it a good brand listing, covering most of the well established houses, and not being limited to premiums only: old-line brand bundle cigars like Don Mateo and Riata are in there, along with Cuban bright lights like Cohiba and Montecristo. The listing includes excellent color photos of the cigars themselves, a listing of many of the size/ring shapes available in each line, and a simple rating scale for flavor and quality that tries to be subjective. Although cigars change wrappers as often as we change cloths, the book is worth having as a superior brand reference.

Oh, they also through in few pages on the history of tobacco, the plight of the Caribbean people, the mechanics of cigar manufacture, standard smoking procedure, and all that. Well, most of that, I made that up about the plight of the people. But if you buy this one, buy it for the brands.

Leads From An Electronic Bookstore

What follows are titles and limited information gleaned from searching at Amazon.com, "Earth's Biggest Bookstore," an Internet bookseller found at, you guessed it, www.amazon.com. Barnes & Noble has one, too, and of course by the time you read this there will be many others.

I've included their current pricing and availability information, 'cause you might want to know. Where descriptions are included, they are from Amazon's web page verbatim, and though they do not cite the ultimate source, I suspect they are the publisher's. You'll note some duplication from the several titles I myself reviewed above; they are repeated to give more complete information. I've excluded some of the more obscure and tangential titles. Here goes:

Antique Cigar Cutters & Lighters
(Schiffer Book for Collectors)
Jerry Terranova, Douglas Congdon-Martin
Hardcover Published 1996
Our Price: $69.95 Ships in 1-2 weeks

Art of the Cigar Label
Joe Davidson / Hardcover / Published 1996
Our Price: $29.98 Usually ships in 24 hours

Synopsis: A history of the growth of the tobacco and lithograph industry offers insights into values, collecting, identifying old cigar labels, and more, and is accompanied by hundreds of color photographs of historically significant labels.

The Book of the Havana Cigar

Brian Innes / Hardcover / Published 1983
(Hard to Find)

The Cigar

Barnaby, III Conrad / Hardcover / Published 1996
Our Price: $20.97 Usually ships in 24 hours

Synopsis: The author of The Martini—an avid fan of cigars himself—has dedicated his new book to the poetic, historical, and artistic pursuit of this wonderful, timeless passion. Drawing upon examples from art, film, literature, and politics, The Cigar presents a lushly illustrated, fascinating social history which honors the cigar's origins and development, as well as its sexy and everlasting allure. 130+ photos, many in color.

Cigar Aficionado's Buying Guide 1997-1998 : Ratings & Prices for More Than 1000 Cigars

Marvin Shanken (Editor) / Paperback /
Published 1997
Our Price: $10.36   Ships in 2-3 days

Synopsis: Churchills, Coronas, Torpedoes, Maduros—which cigar should you smoke and why? Here are ratings and tasting notes for more than 800 cigars, along with a directory of leading tobacconists around the world and profiles of more than 1,300 cigar-friendly restaurants. Full-color photos.

Cigar Almanac

Lew Rothman / Unknown Binding
(Hard to Find)

The Cigar in Art

Terence Conran (Editor), Overlook Press / Hardcover / Published 1997

Our Price: $24.50 Ships in 2-3 days

Synopsis: Picasso, John Singer Sargent, Diego Rivera, and Max Beerbohm are some of the 85 artists represented here, all paying homage to the cigar. Each piece of art is accompanied by a quote or commentary by a cigar aficionado, from Churchill and Freud to today's best-known cigar lovers from the film, art, business, and sports worlds. Like a truly fine cigar, this is a book to be coveted and savored. 85 full-color illustrations.

Cigar Chic : A Woman's Perspective

Tomima Edmark / Hardcover / Published 1995

Our Price: $10.46 Ships in 2-3 days

The Cigar Companion : A Conoisseur's Guide

Anwer Bati / Hardcover / Published 1993

(Hard to Find)

Cigar Cool

Diane, Michael A Belslcy (Editor) / Paperback / Published 1997

Our Price: $9.95 (Special Order)

Cigarette Lighters

(Schiffer Book for Collectors With Value Guide.)
Stuart Schneider, George Fischler / Hardcover / Published 1996

Our Price: $39.95 Ships in 2-3 days

Collector's Guide to Cigarette Lighters

James Flanagan / Paperback / Published 1994

Our Price: $14.36 Ships in 2-3 days

Collector's Guide to Cigarette Lighters : Identification and Values
James Flanagan / Paperback / Published 1996
Our Price: $14.36 Ships in 2-3 days

The Good Cigar
H. Paul Jeffers, et al / Hardcover / Published 1996
Our Price: $17.50 Ships in 2-3 days

Habanos : The Story of the Havana Cigar
Nancy Stout / Hardcover / Published 1997
Our Price: $35.00

Handbook of American Cigar Boxes With Prices
Books and Pamphlets/Signed/
Limited Edition/Registered
Tony Hyman / Hardcover / Published 1979
Our Price: $24.95 (Special Order)

The Handmade Cigar : Collector's Guide & Journal
Tom Connor, Jim Downey / Hardcover /
Published 1997
Our Price: $17.50 Ships in 2-3 days

The Havana Cigar : Cuba's Finest
Charles Del Todesco, et al / Hardcover /
Published 1997
Our Price: $45.50 Ships in 2-3 days
> **Synopsis:** After two years spent in Cuba researching
> the production of the Havana, Del Todesco has pulled
> together a remarkable testament to this legendary
> status symbol of cigars. 76 illustrations, 67 in color.
> Cigar catalog with 295 photos.

Holy Smoke : A Literary Romp Through the History of the Cigar
Guillermo Cobrea Infante, et al / Hardcover /
Published 1997

Our Price: $17.47 ~ You Save: $7.48 (30%)

Synopsis: A definitive celebration of the cigar explores stories about cigars and the people who have smoked them, discussing their history, how they are made, and the importance of the brand and the band, as well as a providing a guide to the manners and mores of cigar smoking.

The Legend of the Lighter

Ad Van Weert, et al / Hardcover / Published 1995
Our Price: $31.50 Ships in 2-3 days

Nat Sherman's a Passion for Cigars : Selecting, Preserving, Smoking, and Savoring One of Life's Greatest Pleasures

Joel Sherman, Robert Ivry / Hardcover /
Published 1996
Our Price: $17.47 Ships in 2-3 days

Synopsis: Renewed interest in one of life's most affordable luxuries—cigars—has grown into a nationwide trend. The demographics aren't just smoke, either— recent estimates indicate as many as ten million Americans are now smoking over 100 million cigars annually. Here Joel Sherman, son of tobacconist Nat Sherman, has created the definitive guide to cigars.

Old-Time Cigar Labels in Full Color : In Full Color

(Dover Pictorial Archive Series)
Carol Belanger Grafton (Editor) / Paperback /
Published 1996
Our Price: $6.36 Ships in 2-3 days

101 Ways to Answer the Request : 'Would You Please Put Out That # (!&!$ Cigar!')

Sean Kelly / Paperback / Published 1987
(Hard to Find)

Perelman's Pocket Cyclopedia of Cigars
Richard B. Perelman / Paperback / Published 1996
Our Price: $9.95 (Special Order)

Key West : Cigar City, U.S.A.
L. Glenn Westfall / Paperback / Published 1984
Our Price: $20.00 (Special Order)

Lighters : Accendini
Stefano Bisconcini (Photographer) / Paperback /
Published 1997
Our Price: $12.95

The Ultimate Cigar Book
Richard Carleton Hacker / Hardcover /
Published 1996
Our Price: $34.95

World's Best Cigars CD-ROM
Samuel Vasquez / CD-ROM / Published 1997
Our Price: $24.99 (Special Order)

Zippo : The Great American Lighter
David Poore / Hardcover / Published 1997
Our Price: $39.95

This last entry was included more for collectibles interest than for guidance in daily smoking, what with those tallow-fire flames, and all.

There you are, folks. All the relevant listings concurred up by the search engines at "Earth's Largest Bookstore." A complete library is only a point n' click away.

CHAPTER TWELVE

Smokin' Up The World Wide Web

Truly, this is a vast land, this "hyperspace," a boundless jungle full of delight, but at every turn ready to suck priceless marketing information out of the very skulls of the unwary who tread there. Pack a machete and a gold card, and have a care.

I won't even try to make this comprehensive. The Web is so big and changes and grows so quickly, that any such completeness will not really matter by the time you read this. But we will give the important sites, of great interest and carrying valuable information. Fortunately, the Web is also full of maps and beacons, in the way of search engines and links, that you should have little trouble finding your way around whatever universe happens to exist there when you get around to it, if you want to go exploring. One final thought: Web pages can spring into being overnight, and, like fireflies, disappear just as quickly. The operator may lose money, get bored with it, change addresses and screw up the "change of address form," or merge himself into another page. So don't be surprised to find new ones and lose old ones. The thing mutates like primordial soup.

There are literally thousands - perhaps tens of thousands - of cigar-related sites on the Web. A causal search using any of the popular engines, like Lycos or InfoSeek, will dredge up far more entries than any but a true webworm (did I coin a term?)

would care to access. Go ahead, try it, bedazzle yourself with the smoking power at your fingertips. We have delved long and deep for you, and give the most promising addresses below. For the most part we have referenced only what we consider to be primary sites, those which are both dedicated mostly to cigars, and serve as good launching points to related sites.

A word on search engines. Recent press has revealed that the web has grown so vast that no single search engine comes close to covering it. In fact, there is very much overlap between what each engine will dredge up with given keywords. If you want to be thorough - and want to spend your vacation this way - use your search parameters with each engine available to you. Just be prepared for tons of references from each...

Magazine Sites

Let's begin with the sites for the two big magazines, C.A. and SMOKE.

Cigar Aficionado

www.cigaraficionado.com

The C.A. site is, like the paper magazine, very slickly laid out, well organized, and powerful. The home page is arranged with a "widebar," containing timely stories, graphics, and features, and a sidebar menu with regular features like "drink," "forums," "cigar ratings," "retailers," "restaurants," "cigar stars," "sports/gaming," "wall street," and so on. Many of these allow you to search databases for items of interest. "the library," a button on the sidebar menu, lets you access and read every article in every issue published, or search for particular parameters. Sadly, it is text only, with no ads or illustrations, but contains a ton of free information. Of course, you can also subscribe, visit a small virtual giftshop, or e-mail in your own taste testing. You can even set up a portfolio and get stock quotes here by hitting the "wall street" button, no doubt getting on all sorts of broker mailing lists in the process. But that's O.K., you run this risk at any Web site. Just don't give out your Social Security number, or your mother's maiden name!

Have a look when you have an hour or so to wander on a rainy night.

SMOKE

www.smokemag.com

The SMOKE page is different from C.A.'s as you might suspect, but well developed, and very interesting. The big part of the page lets you read summaries of articles in the current issue, and get the complete text of selected pieces. You can also access the tables of contents from past issues, read the articles, and, unlike the C.A. site, get high quality pictures and graphics from the individual issues. There's a shopping button to teleport you to the Web sites of cigar-related merchants, and a very comprehensive links button to blow you away from SMOKE to all manner of interesting places, from an airport smoking guide, to chat rooms and even a virtual - and very comprehensive - cigar-band museum! This links facility is especially well constructed, and will take you nearly anywhere but to the C.A. page. SMOKE's page is another great place to while away those rainy evening hours, and a fine alternative to your regular diet of Nickelodeon.

Other Commercial Launch Points

The Tobacconist

www.thetobacconist.com

Another real neat site is "The Tobacconist," a quasi-non commercial collection of launch points run by "your purveyor, Ken Mortensen." By non-commercial I mean that while I'm sure Ken makes money off it - through advertising and stuff like that - the sight is not devoted to any one particular product or vendor. In fact, you will find dozens listed here, like Nat Sherman, J.R., and scores of others. One slipped click and you are in their virtual shops, and their clutches. But you will also find writings and cigar "columns" from all sorts of interesting parties, including an intriguingly- titled one called "Alison Likes Cigars." This site is definitely worth a stop, especially because it is such a well-connected gateway to lots and lots of other good sites. Seventy three launching points, at last count, including vendors. Do drop by and save me the trouble of describing in detail here the sites collected there. The old boy may think he has them all, but he doesn't, as we'll see below. Which is why Ken also provides links to powerful search engines on cigar stuff, including Lycos, Yahoo, and AT&T Search. No need to even type the word "cigar" - just click on the entry. Which is one of the things that makes the Web so fascinating. The smart sites are interconnected like neural central, twisted together like a bucket of writhing snakes; one never know where he wind up, once he jump in.

Columbia Unversity Cigar Society
www.cc.columbia.edu./cu/cigar/links.html
Another collection of links, the Columbia site is much less developed than Ken's as I write, offering as yet only a handful - but different from those found above. Crawl by and have a hit.

The Internet Cigar Group
www.cigargroup.com
Found at the Columbia site, the Internet Cigar Group is a very, very slick site, full of goodies from all over. The sub-headline promotes it as "the home of the Internet Cigar Group - the world's largest organization of cybersmokers! Our pages here are full of free, non-commercial information representing cybersmokers from all over the world!" Despite this, it is chock full of commercial launch points, but still very cool. There are icons for "special deals," college cigar clubs, city

cigar clubs, making your own humidor, cigars and health, smoker events, chat rooms, and 800 telephone number lists. And, of course, yet more links. Well worth a stop.

Fujipub.com Cigar Page
www.netins.net/showcase/fujicig

This is a vast collection of commercial sites - nearly 300 as I smoke and write. After the modest introduction - "Cigars, wines and spirits are our passion and the companies that we have collected at FUJIPUB.COM share that passion. Whether you've been smoking cigars for seventy years or seventy minutes, here you will find the cigar information you are looking for. Maybe that's why NetGuide gave us an unprecedented five stars for cigar content, Smoke Magazine said 'Fuji is unquestionably the most comprehensive starting point for cigars and wine/spirits information on the Internet,' New Riders included us as the only cigar page in The World Wide Web Top 1000, and Point Communication ranked us the number one cigar page on the planet." - you'll find more links than Myrtle Beach. The sites really are too numerous to mention. Every thing from cigar antiques and apparel, to calendars, music (cigar music?), cigar radio, and cigar vacations.

Rather than wear my fingerprints off by typing them all, feast your ash on this cut-and-pasted partial listing:

Main Cigar Page • Cigar Shops • Cigar Brands Cigar Humidors • The BIGLIST • What's New Classic Page • Accessories Shops • Antiques Apparel • Art • Ashtrays • Associations • Books Brands • ...Yes, I know I stopped in mid-B, I ran out of electrons. Go look for yourself. Just kidding, the electron truck just came by. Here's the rest of the electron truck just came by. Here's the rest of the partial list... • Calendars • Carrying Cases • Clocks and Pens • Clubs • COMCs • Cutters • Distributors • Drinks • Events • FAQs • Golf • Holders Humidification Devices • Humidors • IRCs • Lighters • Liquors • Listserves • Magazines • Music Newsgroups • Odor Eliminators • Personalized Gift

Services • Pipes and Tobaccos • Private Labels Radio • Satire • Shops • Society Pages • Software Specials, Promotions & Contests • Spirits • Stocks Vacations • Venues • Videos • Wholesalers • Wine Shops • ...Wheh! I know it seems that some of these can't possibly be cigar related, but they all are. Surf on over. And bring your Mastercard.

Whizstreet "Up in Smoke" Cigar Band Museum Cigar Links

www.mcs.net/~whizstrt/ciglinx.html

Another great set of links, this one is build around a "theme park" whose theme, as you may have surmised, is cigar box/cigar band art. The link at the top of the page to the University of South Florida/Tampa's collection is particularly interesting, full of pretty, fairly high-res examples of mostly American (dare I say Tampaian?) cigar-art. Beyond this, the page describes itself as follows: "In general, because this links list is part of a non-commercial webpage we have made an editorial decision to no longer include links to strictly commercial cigar-related sites, i.e., wholesale or retail sellers of cigars whose sites consist of little more than price lists or sales catalogues.

There are many comprehensive lists of links to cigar vendors and manufacturers already available such as are contained in personal web pages by Eric Campbell or Bob Curtis (listed below), or as can be located by using various Web search engines. We will however continue to selectively include links to certain commercial sites that in our opinion also offer substantive cigar-related information in supplement to their product offerings, or that are otherwise novel or unusual. Any links to commercially oriented sites are provided for reference only."

This site is another great place to gather information and jump off again, a grand link-de- links. It is powerful, well worth a stop, and provides links to good sites which I have not seen elsewhere. Since one of its last listed links is to Fuji (though I don't think you can get here from there), I finally feel as if I am running in great electronic circles, and have given you more than enough information to cut through the haze. Or at least enough to go off blindly into the cyber-fog. There is much to be learned and much fun to be had, tramping about the Internet. To say nothing of the electronic shopping-baskets beyond count. Punch a few keys and see what you turn up.

Cigar Radio

I know this is supposed to be the Web section, and radio is a bit lower-tech, I couldn't resist filching these listings from the Fuji site, 'cause I know you'd what to know. Gosh, I want to know...and didn't until now.

Smoke This!!!

http://smokethis.com/

From the Web page: "The Cigar Connoisseur Radio Network airs from noon to 2PM Eastern every Saturday. If you can't get Smoke This!!! on your local station, call your station and let your voice be heard! Your voice can also be heard on our call in lines at 1-888-SMOKE-THIS. The Cigar Connoisseur Radio Network can be tuned in on the following stations...

Albuquerque	**KHTL**	**Atlanta**	**WCNN**
Buffalo	**WBEN**	**Honolulu**	**KWAI**
Jacksonville	**WZNZ**	**Las Vegas**	**KVEG**
Los Angeles	**KFI**	**Miami**	**WIOD**
Mobile	**WNTM**	**Monterey**	**KNRY**
Orlando	**WWNZ**	**Reno**	**KKOH**
Richmond	**WRVH**	**Sacramento**	**KSTE**
Salt Lake City	**KAPN**	**Seattle**	**KRKO**
Spokane	**KJRB**	**Tallahassee**	**WANM**
Tampa	**WSUN**		

Call the station for exact air times in your area. ALL of the stations listed carry SMOKE THIS!!!"

Lighten Up! Cigar Radio Network

http://cigaradio.com/

Their web page describes the program as: "Lighten Up! broadcasts live from Los Angeles to America's two largest radio markets - New York and Los Angeles - with a combined population of 28.2 million, as well as other significant markets within reach of our program's broadcast signal. Listeners will have the opportunity to call in and speak one-on-one with their favorite celebrities, cigar makers, beautiful models, wine experts, Fortune 500 CEO's, political figures and sports stars who all share a common bond - CIGARS!"

Where: Southern California on 870AM KIEV
When: Saturdays, 12:00p.m. to 1:00p.m.

Where: New York on 1050AM WEUD
When: Saturdays, 3:00p.m. to 4:00p.m.

While in just the two markets, they do have an awfully nice web page, worth a look. And certainly worth a trial listen if you live near one of the big two.

Even if not living in a listed city, both web sites are worth checking, of course, to see if your market has been added. Keep your mouse, and your ears, up.

CHAPTER THIRTEEN

Dr. Camarda's Favorite Brands

I just couldn't help myself. Just couldn't keep my own prejudiced preferences from you. As we have been saying all along,
taste in cigars is a highly personal and subjective thing. But
this is what I like. If your inclination runs to heavier, more
robust smokes with a wide band of flavor, and your tasting
equipment is wired kinda like mine, you may enjoy the following offerings. If not, throttle back to the softer taste of Dominicans, or the flatter flavor of Mexico. And remember always that my tastes are in large part dictated by the shrieking from my wallet.

Punch and Hoyo de Monterrey

For a very long time Villazon's Punch and Hoyo de
Monterrey were my absolute favorite brands. Consistent year
after year, well made, richly flavored and reasonably priced,
the two brands were nearly identical but for Punch being a bit
stronger. In EMS wrapper to me they were superb. I remained
loyal even through the modest price increases that rode the
new wave of bourgeois fashion, and as the wrappers got darker
and darker. I still am when I can find them, but their rarity
has relegated them to the occasional treat category for me now.
I suspect that the maker has "cashed in" and diverted his factories to the manufacture of a host of new super premiums,
and only a trickle of the old brands makes it to market now.

Still very good when you can find them, and you will see them in shops from time to time. I think that they let a few boxes slip out the back door every once in a while just to keep the brand names alive.

Bances

Another Villizon brand, also named for a favorite old Cuban brand, though unlike Punch and Hoya, I don't think they make this one in Cuba anymore. Like those other two, these are made in Honduras and are robust in flavor. Quality is similar, but the lower price point target has made them for years a better buy. Grab 'em when you can get 'em. Supply is tight. And, of course, prices are up.

Excalibur

This is a moderately priced super premium (which means they are still expensive cigars) made by Villizon and based on the Hoyo brand. Very good, with superb construction and taste, these were considered by many to be the best non-Cubans in the world before the cigar boom. Now, there're just another premium. Supply is tight but better than for the Villizon base brands. Worth a try, but remember that you can get a whole bundle of good Hondurans for what three of these babies will cost you. They come in nice boxes, though.

Villizon launched a similar top of the line brand segment called Punch Gran Cru, with high prices and even better boxes. I smoked a couple hundred, but never found them as good as Excaliburs, and never worth the price.

J.R. Ultimates

I'm pretty sure that these are made by Villizon for J.R. Tobacco, along the lines of Excalibur, using the same boxes but perhaps a slightly different blend. Quality - from wrapper, to blend and construction - is excellent, and supply seems to be plentiful. And you can still get any color you want. Prices are extremely reasonable when one considers that these are super premiums: two, three bucks apiece, which is barely the price nowadays for mediocre brands in the average shop. Still expensive when you look at what else you can find in the J.R. candystore, but the choice if you want to invest in a box of once in awhile but still cost-effective treats.

Baccarat

Another Honduran brand, reasonably priced and in good supply. Medium-strong and very sweet, they taste like they have been dipped in sugar water, or otherwise treated. Still good and a nice change of pace.

Joya De Nicaragua

These were just super, rich and strong, before the Sandinistas wrecked the country. The first I tasted after the return of democracy were pretty poor, but quality has been quickly improving. Now good again, they are no longer cheap.

Mocha

Today's mainstay for me, excellent cigars at giveaway prices. Prices at J.R. range from about $11 to $16, depending on size, for the bundle of twenty. In good colors - I was fortunate to pick up 30 or so bundles at the J.R. retail outlet as I passed through North Carolina this summer, and by hand picking I got all light brown. It is tougher to specify shade on the phone, but still worth a try. On the way back down to Florida I cleaned out the store. If you like Hondurans, these are really worth tracking down, and buying in quantity. Hopefully, supply will be constant for awhile. But stock up in case it isn't. The way things are going, these will dry up, and the hunt will go on for the next good five-cent cigar.

Nameless Honduran and Nicaraguan Bundles

This is the land of hit or miss. The cigars come wrapped in clear cello with no markings other than the Honduran tax stamp, and you have no idea what you are getting, and if what you get next time is the same. I know it may look the same. But you don't know.

That said, sometimes you strike gold, and get well made cigars that you even like. And the price is usually low. So take a chance, life is short, and the trash barrel is near.

To me, the Hondurans have consistently offered better taste and value.

Cuban Partagas, Punch, and Hoyo de Monterrey

Cubans, I love you all! I will put up with construction flaws, miser-tight draws, and cigarette-short filler from you, which in other cigars would mean a quick trip to the parts box. But most of you are well made and well behaved. And taste like nothing else.

Cuban Punch and Hoyo de Monterrey are extraordinarily good. I mean to die for, to commit financial suicide. Which is what you will have to do to get them in any quantity. They are grand, but cost too much for me to justify any more than one or two a year.

Cuban Partagas, especially in the medium sizes, are much more reasonably priced, and taste almost as good. If you want - and are willing to pay for - good Cubans, these are the ones to get a box or two of if you have the opportunity to buy them.

Dominican Partagas

These are very well made, on the expensive side, and strong for a Dominican cigar. Which means light to medium strong, in my mouth. I buy them when a vendor, like a hotel or restaurant - offers only Dominicans, and I really want a cigar.

A. Fuente

Now one of the largest makers, this Dominican company produces a dazzling array of lines and models. They also blend in a good bit from other countries. The heavier varieties, like Opus, Gran Reserva, and Hemmingway, approach Honduran and Nicaraguan strength. Still light to me, I smoke them for a very occasional change of pace, or when they are the only decent cigars to be found in the joint.

Don Mateo

An old-line "bundle brand," price and quality have remained good - and consistent - for a long time. Good construction, heavy and flavorful, these Hondurans seem to always be in good supply, and prices have not risen much. You can still get good sizes for under $20 the bundle of 25 from some sources, a bit more elsewhere. I've been smoking a lot of these lately.

Favorite Sizes

I prefer medium ring, medium length cigars, ring of 40-46 and 5 to 6 inches long. Not only do I find the best buys here, but the smoking length is usually right for me, with the thickness allowing for adequate diversity of blend. Yes, diversity is important, both politically correct and a sign of good taste.

Thinner smokes, like panatelas, are nice, give a very elegant look, and can be surprisingly strong for their small bore, but are prone to draw problems. Good ones are great, but I'm mostly a corona man these days.

I like big cigars, too, but have been turned off by the frequency of burn and draw problems I've encountered in these expensive products.

One the whole, medium sizes are just right for this baby bear.

Favorite Colors

Medium shades, too, whether you call it Claro, light brown, EMS, or natural. As mentioned earlier, I find these to taste more consistently stronger and deeper than the more macho-looking Maduro ranges. Not that dark brown can't taste very strong and rich, as it does regularly in Cubans. But in the rest of the Caribbean, I find the dark too often a tease, and have stopped chasing them. Just a modest tan for me now, please. And, inexplicably, I encounter fewer construction and draw problems in the lighter cigars. I have no idea why this should be, but it be for me. I wind up throwing too many of the darker ones away, even before I get a chance to sample their flat taste. Likely just a coincidence.

Green is also sometimes good. Spicy, sweet, lighter and more delicate than brown, with a hint of springtime and fresh-cut grass. Too much so for a steady diet, but nice from time to time. Green also seems to be more plug resistant than Maduro. Or so I think.

Final Warning!

Of course, all of this reflects my own highly subjective tastes. You must seek and see for yourself. Plus the brand situation is in such torrid flux that you'll have to hunt around the markets and see what happens to be around when you want to buy, if you want to get good value. And, of course, there are far, far more than we have listed above. This is just the handful of my favorites. Most of the major, old line brands will always be there, hopefully not at ever spiraling prices.

Just today my brother-in-law Bill told me that his brother-in-law Scott gave this lament: "Every time I go to buy my favorite cigars, they cost a dollar more each. Even at only one a day, I just can't afford $6, $7, even $8 for a smoke! What will I do?" Read this book, Scottie-boy. There'll be a copy under your tree this year.

Just like I promised you at the Dinosaur B-B-Q in Syracuse.

CHAPTER FOURTEEN

Strictly For Women

All right, guys, I know that you are the predominant readers of this book. But new federal regulations have mandated a one-chapter literary set-aside for female content in books with primarily male themes. You wouldn't want me to lose my Library of Congress Card privileges, would you? To say nothing of the chauvinist impact fees...which would double the cost of the book alone, and get me banned by Lord-knows-how-many activist groups.

The last thing I want is a parade of woman protesters marching back and forth in front of my window. Right?

So...please? Grab a beer and wait in the next chapter? I'll be right along.

Still there? Out, already! Want to complain about reverse-male-discrimination? Try and get a NOW application, or something, if you want to make a statement. Believe me, you'll feel a whole lot better about yourself tomorrow if you don't look.

ଔ   ଔ   ଔ   ଔ   ଔ   ଔ   ଔ   ଔ

There, then, ladies. We're alone. Let the brutes whine in the next chapter. Some will salivate and cavort like dogs, it is true. It is their nature, poor things. But some matters are best left between just us, after all. Don't you think?

This chapter will serve two purposes. One, to introduce you to the gentle pleasure of cigar smoke, if you have a yen, from a perspective as close to your own as I can approach. Second, to shop for cigars for the man (or men) in your life, if you are so inclined.

Cigar Smoking Tips for Women

The first thing I really must do is refer you to <u>Cigar Chic : A Woman's Perspective</u> by Tomima Edmark, which is, of course, all about teaching women about cigars. Ms. Edmark is also the author of a book on the fine art of kissing, called <u>365 Ways to Kiss Your Love</u>, and I'll leave that just as it is. Here is a whole book on the subject, if you wish to move beyond my own coarse advice. Take it with a bottle of nail-polish remover, though. For instance, she gives advice on preventing the subtle aroma of cigar smoke from lingering on one's fingertips...which to me is less of a concern than the fact that cigar-breath will knock down a mailbox at ten paces. So perhaps a trot through the other chapters in my own book will give some measure of balance.

<u>Cigar Selection for Women</u>

This is a delicate subject. I know that some of you are stronger than many men. I know some ladies that can bench-press more than I can, and I've been working out for decades. And all of you are stronger in many important ways, like getting multiple things done, keeping going when ill, and keeping your head in difficult situations. As Robert Heinlein said, "Men are more sentimental than women. It blurs their thinking." He also said "I came, I saw, she conquered..."

So forgive me if I suggest that in this, your tastes might run a bit more to the, ah, refined than my own, and suggest that you start with something a bit less overwhelming in flavor. Afterwards, if you want to work your way up to the kind of tobacco-scrapings and-Elmer's glue taste that coats your tongue in middle-weight-resin, so be it. That's how most men work up to it, anyway.

I would suggest you begin with the really light stuff. Jamaican. Maybe Canary Islands. The very lightest of the Dominicans. Of the old-line names, Macacudo, Royal Jamaica, and Don Diego would be good bets.

Avoid, until you are ready to wade deeper, stronger stuff, as that from Honduras, Cuba, and Nicaragua tends to be. In my opinion, this is where the real flavor is. But tread lightly. It can be overpowering for a newcomer.

I say this not only to enhance your pleasure, but to protect your immediate health, as well. The best example of this I can give you is of my old friend and buddy from my stock-brokerage days, Tim aka Buckwheat. Tim at that time had been a lifelong cigarette smoker. At his bachelor party in NY, after a few, he asked for one of my standard Hondurans. Of course, I obliged. Mind you this fellow was acclimated to nicotine. Anyway, after a few minutes of puffing, he headed off to the loo to, ah, clear his palate. The fellow turned near-green and almost ruined the evening's festivities for himself. His tastes have since matured and he buys the heavy stuff for himself now. But beginners must be careful.

For similar reasons, I consul thin cigars, to start. Aside from the fact that the slender shape compliments a woman's appearance better (and is less phallic, but that is another issue, and gets - almost! - its own section), thinner cigars simply emit less powerful smoke. Length (at least in this) is not nearly as much of an issue, but shorter ones cost less, and don't smoke for as long a time. And you may want to limit smoking time, to start.

On wrapper color, I suggest, for you, Maduro, the dark-brown, almost-black ones. Most of these are milder, in my experience. You may also like the (now hard-to-find) candela, or green, which smokes lighter and sweeter. The darker ones will probably look better "on" you.

If for some reason you haven't been through the rest of the material in this book, have a look at the following section, "Selecting Cigars for Men," for a quick primer on buying cigars. Remember my advice on size and countries, though.

Preparing the Cigar to Smoke

Not much to it, really. First we must puncture the cap, so as to allow smoke to pass through. This is well covered in the chapter on "Smoking Mechanics," so I won't repeat it here. Though an interesting variation, and a flirty one, would be to make an incision in the head with your fingernail, or perhaps several in order to remove a flap of tobacco. I'll have to leave it to you to determine if the tensile strength of a fingernail is up to this sort of use, though judging from the occasional scratches which have been so inflicted (for a variety of reasons) on my skin, I'll bet it is.

I do, however, suggest that you avoid my favorite technique, which is gently nibbling the end off with your teeth. You are liable to make quite an impression if you do and one which you may not want to make. If you do, consider the ideas in the "On Teasing Men with Your Cigar" section, below. To show why, here's the "teeth" technique partially copied from the "...Mechanics" section: "Wrapper tobacco is delicate, and must be approached much like a woman. Begin by gently nibbling and tugging on the cap, a bit out from the center. Whisper as the cap begins to yield. The point is to soften and carefully tear...softly bite and tug at the same time, and a section of cap will slide off, leaving a not quite perfect hole, but big enough for good draw, and with enough cap remaining to hold things together."

Sorry, couldn't resist. But you can imagine the impression that might make if you are not alone. And there is the risk of getting bits of tobacco stuck in one's teeth to consider.

Actually Smoking the Darn Thing

Lighting and all that has already been covered in detail in the preceding chapters.

Here's the short version. Wooden match or butane lighter only. Gently rotate the cigar in the flame as you puff to ensure even lighting, and puff-in-flame until the entire tip clearly glows. Use a mirror to tell, or take the cigar out of your mouth to check. Once lit, you should puff at least every few minutes or so, to keep it going. Few things taste as bad as re-lighting a cigar that's been permitted to go out and cool off. Don't listen to anyone else on this. Trust me. The foul taste of a once-smoked cigar will ruin your evening. This comes from a mouth jaded to cigar smoke. Believe it.

Smoke until you've had enough, or the flavor begins to noticeably harsh-en. This happens because the cigar acts as its own filter and tars and other stuff accumulate with increasing concentration in the tobacco remaining as the cigar get shorter. Most folks begin to notice this with between half and one-third of the cigar left. Throw it away when it begins to taste bad. As for saving any unused portion for later, again, forget it. Better you should smoke dried sunflowers. Once a cigar is dead - and it is dead once permitted to go out and cool down - it is dead. Smoking it will just make you sick, or at least gag unpleasantly. I only stress this because I care.

Which brings us to the delicate topic of how to hold your cigar. Balance it on your middle finger and hold it there, gently, with your forefinger. Or alternate between thumb and middle finger as the resting point. A few minutes practice with an unlit cigar - or a pencil, for that matter will give you the trick.

Keep it in your mouth only to puff, supported by your hand. Actually holding it with your lips requires more force than you may imagine, and will create a look best reserved for the next section. Save clenching the beast between teeth only for the most special occasions.

When the cigar is finished, set it down in an ashtray, or some other non-flammable surface where it can sit for awhile until it goes out by itself. <u>Do not</u> try and snuff it out like a cigarette. This will just make a huge mess and produce more unwanted smoke than you will believe.

On Teasing Men with Your Cigar

You who venture here, know that a large cigar in the mouth of a woman is a most sensual thing. Heck, even in her hand, it is pretty sexy. Can't help it, just is. Don't blame me. I did not make things the way they are. I just try and enjoy them.

So select your cigar sizes with this in mind.

For those of you who <u>want</u> to occasionally project this message, you really need little instruction from me. Fondle the cigar, more than hold it. Keep changing the position in your hand. Bring it to your mouth often and rotate the cigar as you puff. Tap the cigar slowly to ash it, more of a stroke than a tap, perhaps while gazing into some lucky fellow's eyes. Look away as if embarrassed to have discovered yourself doing this. Expel the smoke with a sensual flourish, slowly, gazing off into the distance. You get the idea. Heck, you should probably tell me.

Do all of this with an air of complete innocence, as if entirely unaware of the imagery you create.

Be prepared for some pretty serious notice among the men in the crowd. And, perhaps, from the women with them, as well - but watch out in the ladies room!

Selecting Cigars for Men

This section is designed to be a micro-mini course in cigar selection, for those of you who want to just get something nice for a cigar smoker in your life, without really wanting to learn more than is necessary to do that.

To begin with, "drugstore" mass-produced cigars are out. You want something handmade and imported. Handmade will appear somewhere on the packaging, usually on the cigar band. This is good, since this type of cigar is usually purchased singly, or at least one at a time. Be prepared to spend anywhere from two to five dollars apiece if you shop causally. You can get good cigars cheaper ($.75 or less, like the one I'm smoking now), but you need to know more to do so safely. Forget paying more than $5, no matter how much the clerk extols the virtues of a particular brand.

Cigars imported from these countries, in no set order, are most likely to please: Jamaica, Honduras, Nicaragua, the Dominican Republic, and Cuba. Stick to these.

Unless you know well the tastes of the lucky devil getting the gift (and it may be likely that he doesn't know his own tastes very well yet, either), be safe and get a small assortment if buying more than one. Buying a box at today's prices without knowing exactly what the fellow likes is too risky. He may never tell you, but the box may sit around for a long time. Better to spread your bets and get a little of each. Some from each country mentioned, perhaps some dark brown, and some lighter brown. For size, stick with medium (about six inches long and half an inch wide), or get several different sizes. Maybe wrap the little assortment with a ribbon and include some good wooden matches - the shop should give you a small box of matches with the cigars. The cigars should be given to you in a zip-lock-type bag to preserve freshness. Ask your fellow to keep track of which ones he enjoys best as he smokes, so you will both know for future reference.

As to where to shop, tobacco shops with walk-in humidors (usually look like a walk-in closet with a sliding-glass door) are your best bet. Large liquor stores often have these nowadays, as well, but be prepared for less-than-knowledgeable staff.

Follow these simple rules and you'll be amazed at how well appreciated your thoughtful gift will be.

And with that, our thoughtful tour on this summer's eve of the smoother side of life is at an end.

Thank you for taking the time to read with me. I tried hard to make it informative and enjoyable for you. If you read this for some fellow, I hope that he realizes how lucky he is.

If you read it for yourself, you must be smokin'! I just wish I could watch you do it.

Ciao!

We now return to our brutal male programming. Gentlemen, you may growl, and beat your chest anew. The ladies have let you out.

CHAPTER FIFTEEN

Dr. Camarda's Favorite Spirits And Other Cigar Beverages

Some stuff goes good together. Some stuff don't. When smoking cigars, stay away from milk (as W.C. Feilds said, "are you trying to poison me?"), orange juice, and Pepto-Bismol. But do try with some of the suggestions that follow. You will find many that will enhance the experience, or at least get you so drunk that what little of it you do recall will seem nice. Bear one rule in mind: cigar smoke, even from the lightest Jamaican, is a flavorful thing. To get any synergy you must combine it with another powerful taste. Mineral water will wash your mouth, perhaps clear the palate, but will not compliment a cigar. And remember that W.C. also said., "Don't drink the water. Fish f*** in it." Ditto for Gatoraid, passionfruit juice, and light wines like Lambrusco, Beaujolais, and Ripple. To get a good match, put two heavyweights in the ring of your mouth. Think hearty. Take a big bite.

Coffee

We're not talking about your garden variety thinly brewed "American" coffee here, but the potent brews usually lumped under the "espresso" flag. Stuff like Cuban coffee, Turkish coffee, the strong, thick stuff served in a shot-glass-sized cup. And, of course, that high pressure, foamy-frothed miracle, espresso itself.

This is probably the best beverage-compliment of cigars that I know of. Not only can it be enjoyed at any time without fear of alcoholic fog, but these things really, really taste good together. The powerful taste of this coffee washes the cigar taste away, and replaces it, for a moment, with an equally powerful and complex but different and delightful taste. And then back to the cigar and so on.

I prefer my espresso "straight up," without sugar or anything. But then, I like strong things, and prefer not to deaden their strength. For those that feel otherwise, or are new to this potent brew, a bit of sugar and lemon might improve it for you. Or you might start with one of the "milkshake" variants, like cappuccino, or café latte. These are still strong but softer and delicious and very cigar friendly in their own right. Just don't let them put any whipped creme on it!

Beer

Beer is also good, but you must feel like drinking in order to enjoy it while smoking. Beer is also the best alcoholic choice if you want to be drinking a lot, or for awhile, since the others are too strong to spell you for long, with the possible exception of wine. The "hard liquor" choices must be sipped neat to produce cigar synergy; if you mix drinks, you might as well have a bottle of Yoo-Hoo between your legs, for all it will add to the smoking experience. If you are like me, you can enjoy several beers with a couple cigars of an evening, and still be lucid. Straight liquor is simply too potent for sustained drinking: either your drink won't last long, or you won't.

As with the coffees, the stronger is better rule applies to beer. By strong, we mean taste, and not ethanol concentration. Not that many a pleasant summer afternoon has not been spent in a bass boat, drinking Bud Lite and smoking stogies. But the stronger stuff goes better if you want to focus on the flavor.

German pilsners are a good place to start. Clear, rich, and complex, these make beautiful cigar-mates. Good ones easy to find in the States are Beck's and St. Pauli Girl. Some of the British ales, like Bass, can also be very nice. You might try also some uncut stout, like Guinness, on a snowy evening. As well as the heavier Canadian offerings, particularly Molsen Export Ale, and Brador.

The U.S. has enjoyed such a microbrewery explosion as to give you endless choice of hearty beer and ale. Try first the old favorites, like Sam Adams and Anchor Steam, and branch out from there. But for purity, clarity, and sharp taste - punctuation, no one beats the Germans.

So !Achtung!, baby!, already!

Only one important rule for serious beer drinking. Use a glass, or mug. Always. The flavor is greatly enhanced by letting the brew breath as you quaff, and by not restricting your mouth to a bottle top. And you look so much more thoughtful and distinguished with a stein in your hand, instead of a Coors can.

Though I feel a bit of a cad to type this with a Beck's bottle foaming at my side.

Wine

As much as I like whites, the heavier reds are what really sing in the cigar choir. Dry, deep, complex old things like California cabernets, Italian chiantis, and the stouter stuff from almost any chateau in Bordeaux or Burgundy. A good wine like this, along with a fine cigar, can make for a sublime experience. Remember to let the red breath for an hour or so before you drink it, and take small sips between puffs, gently swirling, sloshing, and mixing the wine with air in your mouth. Small sips, because gulping this stuff through the course of a Churchill can slosh you quicker than you may realize. You may also want to have a bit of mineral water around, to rehydrate the mouth during the dual arid assault of dry smoke and dry wine.

If you insist on whites, because your mate (like mine) insists on them, and you don't want to drink a bottle by yourself, at least go with dry, more complex ones. Real French Chablis. Italian Soave. Varietals like chardonnay, and pinot gregio. Not so good as reds with cigars, but better than Diet Coke, and a clearer head in the morning.

Whiskey

As we enter the realm of hard liquor, it is less important to insist on strongly flavored material, merely because the high percentage of ethanol (an organic solvent) makes quite an impression by itself on your tongue, thank you very much. But many of us look for some flavor beyond this, so we will focus on the more distinct stuff anyway.

The first whiskey that comes to mind, of course, is Scotch. Single malt or blended, nearly any decent brand will complement cigars nicely. It is all a matter of your taste and your pocketbook.

It is unfortunate that my own first Scotch sampling experience, at the age of 13 or so, has in large measure ruined this spirit for me. As much as I try to reacquire the taste, with limited success, I can not entirely shake the body-memory of that first night spent embracing the toilet in Port Jefferson. I do try, but it is hard.

Perhaps for that reason, a love of single-malts has always eluded me. I get on just fine with the blended stuff, but still struggle with Glen Retchin. I promise to try again every once in awhile, though.

Bourbon and Sour Mash whiskey can be nice, as can the smoother rye or Canadian. Start with your favorite, don't mix but sip neat, and take it slow! Just a drop or so rolled on the tongue between puffs will do. Any faster, and both you and your cigar will be found as casualties in the morning, both spent well before their time. Please apply this advice to all of the spirits, if you would avoid seeing things that are not there, and giving the cat some chance of retribution as you lay in compromised state.

Rum

Any will do, but the darker, more complex types like Mayer's are best. Rum is still thought mostly of as a mixing liquor, but has a wonderful taste on its own, and is great with cigars. The hint of molasses-sweetness makes a fine counterpoint to cigar smoke, and you can sing Yo! Ho! Ho! as you smoke, and pretend (like you always wanted to) that you are a Pirate of the Caribbean, as the "tour" boats go crawling by. Again, please use sparingly, and lose the eye patch.

Cordials

These also are wonderful with cigars. The brands and flavors are endless, so try what you like already. Some of my favorites are Amaretto, Grand Marnier, and Frangelica. Sambuca is also nice, as is that lovely yellow Neapolitan liqueur. Sip lightly, roll gently on the tongue, and imagine yourself on a balcony overlooking the French Quarter.

Manhattan Special

This last entry is a delightful coffee soda that I remember from my days growing up near New York City. I am sure they still make it, but finding it may be hard, but worth a try when in N.Y. Try the Italian-specialty grocery stores, the places where they sell grating cheese in five-pound hunks, "Kiss Me! I'm Italian!" aprons, and ten-gallon pasta pots. This stuff is rich and complex without being overly sweet and just grand with a cigar if you want something cold and without alcohol. Try one and you'll lug a case home with you.

CHAPTER SIXTEEN

The True-CIGAR MASTER'S
Trial-by-Smoke Test

1) George Burns said
   1. "If I cannot smoke in Heaven, then I shall not go."
   2. "Gentlemen, you may smoke."
   3. "If I paid that much for a cigar, I'd have to make love to it first."
   4. "White Owls are hard to catch!"

2) With regard to health, smoking cigars
   1. Is proven to make you live longer.
   2. Probably does not matter either way.
   3. Presents at least some slight health risk.
   4. Is about as safe as holding your breath while scuba diving.

3) The width of the cigar matters most to
   1. Satisfying your oral "g" spot.
   2. The women in your life.
   3. The depth and complexity of flavor which can be achieved.
   4. The maximum distance between the tips of extended thumb and forefinger.

4)   The length of the cigar matters most to
   1. The impression you make in the shower.
   2. Your tailor.
   3. How long you can smoke without scorching your fingers.
   4. The period of a pendulum.

5)   Generally, "hand made" means
   1. Final satisfaction after a lonely night.
   2. A manicurist.
   3. Roughed-out by machine and finished by hand.
   4. Craft projects again!

6)   "Totmente a mano," or completely by hand means
   1. A lonely life.
   2. The epitome of self-reliance.
   3. Just what it says.
   4. A pretty good date in high school.
   5. Blindness beckons.
   6. A fan of the Village People.

7)   Wrapper color
   1. There is no difference between colors. We are all the same cigars.
   2. Should be selected to match your outfit.
   3. Makes a big difference in taste and gives the cigar much of its flavor.
   4. They all looks pretty much the same to me.

8)   Generally, the most flavorful, strongest cigars come wrapped
   1. In aluminum foil.
   2. In wax, with a fuse sticking out.
   3. In medium-brown wrappers.
   4. With a tiny bit of garlic pinned to the band.

9)   The binder
   a. Is impossible to retrieve once the seller has accepted your offer.
   b. Is the amount of money you will lose on divorce.
   c. Is the thick, heavy part, under the wrapper, which holds the whole thing together.
   d. Is the fellow who made this book.

10) Most cigars you will see with "Cuba" or "Havana" in their name
   a. Are made with Cuban tobacco on rafts in Caribbean.
   b. Are made with Cuban tobacco in garages in Detroit.
   c. Contain absolutely no Cuban tobacco.
   d. Are rolled by Fidel himself.

11) Cuban seed means
   a. A young fellow destined to do the mamba and call himself "Ricky."
   b. Communist activists who have infiltrated the U.S.
   c. Nothing, really, at all.
   d. The cigar in your hand is the great, great, great, great, great, great great, grandchild of a pre-Castro Punch who was burned in the Revolution.

12) To be safe, Cuban cigars should be purchased
   a. From anyone on the street who hails you as amigo!
   b. Right off the boat, but carry heavy metal. Loaded and cocked.
   c. While (astride?) abroad, from a dealer you trust.
   d. Only in Full Body Rubber.

13) To tell real Habanos from the many counterfeits
   a. Insist on a green card for the cigars.
   b. Be sure to pay cash.
   c. Look for high quality of manufacture and packaging...and smoke one first!
   d. Ask the smuggler to show you the "secret code" on the tax stamp.

14) For quality, only buy product made
    a. By the friendly cigar-roller in St. Augustine.
    b. With pipe tobacco glued together with E-Z Wider.
    c. In Cuba, Nicaragua, Honduras, Jamaica, or Dominica.
    d. In Southeast Asia where labor costs next to nothing.

15) The strongest cigars come from
    a. Grandma's kitchen.
    b. Gold's Gym.
    c. Cuba, Nicaragua, & Honduras.
    d. Fermentation in kerosene, but burn off the light aromatics first.

16) The best point-of-sale guidance will be found
    a. When you are pointing a weapon.
    b. Between 10 and 4, when her husband is at work.
    c. In tobacco shops.
    d. No where. Throw a dart and hope for the best.

17) The best value will be found
    a. Between 5 and 6pm, when the hooker is still fresh but before the rush hits.
    b. In the inner city.
    c. At the mail order houses which deal in heavy volume.
    d. No where. Throw a dart and hope for the best.

18) Freshness in a cigar is best determined by
    a. Giving it a squeeze and seeing if it smiles or slaps.
    b. The date code.
    c. Resiliency and a slight softness.
    d. Lack of putrid odor.

19) To keep cigars fresh, one must provide an environment of
    a. Chastity and classical music.
    b. Led Zeppelin, thick air, and willing companions.
    c. About 70 degrees F and 70% relative humidity.
    d. Top soil, constant drizzle, and gentle breeze.

20) The best humidors have
    1. Your initials carved in their lids.
    2. A secret condom-catch in their bottoms.
    3. A tight seal to keep the moisture in.
    4. Political connections all over the country.

21) When preparing the head to smoke, one must
    1. Consult a Rabbi.
    2. Consult a Priest.
    3. Remove enough of the cap to let smoke pass freely, while still leaving enough to hold the cigar together.
    4. Spin it at least six times and have it kissed by whomever it winds up pointing at.

22) Besides teeth, the best head-slicing tool is
    1. Your butcher.
    2. Your wife.
    3. A guillotine cutter.
    4. The drill-press you remember from the simpler days in metal shop.

23) To light a cigar, it is best to use
    1. Propane.
    2. Natural gas.
    3. A butane lighter or wooden match.
    4. Your own gas (but refer to "3" above to light it).

24) Once a cigar has gone out and cooled, it is best to
    1. Return it to your Egyptian humidor.
    2. Have it sniffed by my doctor-friend.
    3. Discard and disown it.
    4. Try and trade it in at the liquor store.

25) To put a cigar out, you should
    1. Ask first for cigarette and blindfold.
    2. Grind it convincingly under-heel on the marble floor.
    3. Set it in an ashtray and let it expire by itself.
    4. Hand it to a buddy and head to the restroom.

Hang tight! Only five more!
And I bet you have a big score!

26) The written material generally credited with igniting the cigar boom is
   1. What you see on the gas station bathroom walls.
   2. My own humble work.
   3. Cigar Aficionado.
   4. The Time-Life series "tobacco through the ages."
   5. High Times.

27) The chapter "Strictly for Women" produced some remarkable insights, including
   1. A cigar by itself is a most lonely thing.
   2. "I can help you with that, honey."
   3. Don't know, didn't look, no flowers for me!
   4. "You mean they try to look innocent?"

28) The best buys in cigar are most often found in
   1. Your local grocers.
   2. Your local convenience store, the ones where the attendant holds up six fingers and says, "Buy three, get one free!"...or was that "Would you like to buy four for the price of nine?"
   3. Bundles that are marked "hand made," from your favorite country.
   4. Your local Discount-Mart, from whence your love comes saying "you can't believe how many I got for $5!"

29) If you must buy super-premium cigars, you are best to
   1. Save the bands, to impress your friends again with "drug-store" cigars.
   2. Engage the services of a cigar broker you trust.
   3. Stick to the old-line, established brands.
   4. Send me cash and I promise to get you the very cream before I tell anyone else.

30) If you must smuggle Cubans back into this country, you should
   a. Let them drive the pick-up truck. You huddle in the back with green-card-in-wallet, grinning like Letterman.
   b. Contract out their labor before paying them.
   c. Hide 'em in your laundry and walk through Customs like you were Hillary Clinton.
   d. Get them to sign the deed over to their beach house in Cuba before they get on the boat.

Scoring

Alright...let's score this monster. There were exactly 30 questions...the first thing I want you to do is add up your numeric score...just add up the numbers next to each of your answers. Then multiply by 1.111... (the "1"'s go on forever, you remember. Put a bar over it.)

BIG HINT...The "right" answer was always #3! Like you didn't know. So a "perfect" score gives you 100, if you got all three's (3x30x1.111...=100).

Once you get this number (<u>and you fail automatically if you actually do the math</u>), apply it to the following scale:

120+ .... You don't smoke cigars because you really enjoy them, do you? There is another reason, isn't there?

101-119 .... Very good...you have learned much, tobacco-leaf-hopper.

100 .... **YOU** are the **CIGAR-MASTER!** **YES!** **YOU!** Light it up!

80-99 .... Good job, you've picked most of it up. Just remember: bundles! Buy bundles!

79 or less ..... It's OK, just a quiz, right? You'll do much, much better in the test of the tobacco shop. Forget about that girl's chapter. I know you didn't look.

To Boldly Smoke Where No Being Has Smoked Before

A list of target sites for the truly audacious:

- The ladies room.
- The health club.
- While skydiving.
- While scuba diving.
- At the airport in any Middle-Eastern country. Just watch your hands.
- At the airport in Frankfurt, as you are eased outside by the grease-gun-toting security agent.
- In the first-class section of your non-smoking flight.
- In your company's computer room, the one where you have to put on a space suit to enter.
- On the subway platform, but not too close to the tracks.
- At the wedding reception you crash while at an out-of-town hotel.
- On a tour of NASA, while insisting on being addressed as "senator, gosh dammit!"
- While negotiating anything from a position of strength.
- After giving up on negotiations, but before leaving the table.

- In the office of the publisher who declined to buy The Sensible Cigar Connoisseur, saying "there's no such thing." With feet on desk, perhaps while engaged in flatulence.
- On anyone else's boat.
- While playing bridge with in-laws-to-be.
- Your own wedding.
- Your divorce mediation once clear it will turn out badly.
- Piccadilly Circus in the rain, while some new chum asks if you want pubbing?
- On the steps of your local American Cancer Society office.
- At a NOW rally.
- In a bar while your wife is giving birth.
- With your mistress while your wife is giving birth.
- On your divan while your husband cleans the house.
- On your divan while your husband cleans your _____.
- Any park in Dallas.
- At a one table smoking section you pay the maitre d' enough to create especially for you.
- Any bar in California.
- In the Clinton White House.
- In the shower.
- In someone else's shower.
- In your own home?

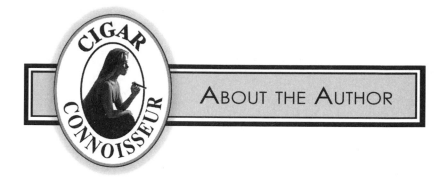

Jeff Camarda began smoking cigars at the age of fourteen or so, primarily due to the influence of his father, Russell, and Uncle Sammy. This was some years after he began smoking cigarettes on an occasional basis, which was primarily the result of the socialization forces at play on young minds at the time. I, I mean he, also ascribes his taste for alcohol to the "real men" of the movies who remarkably could slam down numerous shots before noon, and still go on to save the world later in the day, with nary a neuron mis-firing. Ah, well, we are often the victims, er, captives, of our own experiences.

Who am I kidding here? It is I, not he! Who do you think writes these damn author's bios, anyway? Look at the facts: 1) authors write, and 2) they should know themselves better than anyone else could, right, therapy aside? So what publisher in his right mind is gonna pay to have some third party write this stuff? Now you know.

So can we, please, drop that particular pretense, just this once? This is, after all, a rather lighthearted, straight-shooting book. OK? I promise to stay true to that third-person-subterfuge for my more serious books, but let us, just this once, be up-front. It will be an unusual bio, but an interesting one, I think.

So where was I? Drinking and smoking at 14? Or just smoking, anyway? Through my teens I mostly smoked "drug-store" cigars, Garcia y Vega, A&C, that sort of thing, with the occasional treat of a quality cigar like Royal Jamaica donated by my uncle Sammy from his humidor in Brooklyn, or purchased at the tobacco store in that spanking-new innovation of the local mall. I developed a lifelong interest in quality cigars as a stockbroker in my mid-20's in New York, and began their serious study. Sampling the product in various shops, I found I preferred the heavier taste of Hondurans, which continues to this day. Somehow I got a-hold of a JR catalog in the early 80's, and my pursuit of the good-on-the-cheap began in earnest. I built a 10-gallon aquarium humidor - cutting the glass top myself - and for many years it stayed full of Punch, Flor de Carib, JR Alternatives, and other good Honduran brands which in those days could be had very reasonably. A major cigar coup was buying out the cigar stock of a failed tobacco shop in upstate NY - my eternal thanks to Joel, "The Tobacco Man." After closing his shop, Joel continued via the mail, and supplied pipe tobacco to my father-in-law for some time. Which is how I learned how he cursed me when I finally started buying direct from JR. Oh, well, thanks anyway, Joel!

Got my first taste of Cubans in Hong Kong in 1987 at a business convention, and have eagerly sought out the rich red leaves ever since when out of the country. Red because of the politics, not because I insist on colorado in Cubans.

Anyway, since then I have gone through literal truckloads of hand-made cigars, mostly from Central America, and with rare exception all purchased for far less than the going rate. At this moment I puff on a very good Don Mateo, for which I grudgingly gave a buck to my old pal Sandy at the Tobacco Village. In that time I have devoured everything written I could find on cigars, and learned quite a bit through experimentation on my own.

Besides cigars, I do what these days is called "financial planning." I'm tempted at this point to lapse back into third person, so as not so sound too pompous in reporting my professional credentials, but will not yield. If you have gotten this far in the book, I guess you have forgiven that in me.

I became a stockbroker in 1984 and after a year or so became one of the very top producers in my national firm. In '86 I was asked to become a brokerage manager and passed the NASD series 24 Principal's exam. I still maintain both licenses now. They asked me to open an office for the firm in DC. Seeing the way clear from the salt on the roads for the first time in my life, I bought my first and only Porsche (still drive it) and headed directly from the showroom to the state line. Didn't stop till I got to Virginia. Flew back up to NY, packed the family in the Volvo, and headed to our new life in Dixie.

I got tired of actually running a brokerage office within a few months, especially resenting the time away from my clients and family that baby-sitting 30 or so brokers required. I also tired quickly of Virginia's state income tax (as bad as NY's), personal property tax (like paying sales tax on your car every year), and winter weather. Anne and I took numerous fact-finding trips to southeastern cities over a year or so, looking for a new home in the sun. We settled on Jacksonville, Florida: near the ocean, four seasons (but three pass quickly!), nice size (though it's growth now reminds me of Long Island in the '70's), and NO STATE INCOME TAX!

Here I worked as a broker for awhile, but began to yearn to provide more comprehensive levels of service to financial clients. In 1990 I began study toward the Certified Financial Planner (CFP) designation, and was licensed in 1992. Thereafter I studied for and obtained the Chartered Financial Consultant (ChFC) and Chartered Life Underwriter (CLU) designations, then entered the doctoral program in finance through LaSalle University. Got my Ph.D. in '96 or so and am now enrolled in the Chartered Financial Analyst program, where I am considered "CFA level II candidate," which means I've passed the first of three grueling exams...and think I should have my head examined, instead.

The book in your hands is the second I have written. The first, based on my dissertation, is called <u>Wealth Health</u>, and is the only comprehensive guide to financial planning written in "lay" terms currently available. It is also quite a hoot to read. Not as irreverent as the cigar book (we are talking about money, after all, so show some respect), but I have tried - succeeded, they tell me - to engage the reader in a humorous way to keep them interested and get them to learn this vital stuff - stuff which can save their financial lives. Here's how the sub-title goes, to give you an idea of what's in it:

How to Painlessly and Enjoyably Map Out Your Retirement, Plan Your Estate, Take Care of Your Kids, Protect Your Assets, Cut Your Taxes to the Bone, and Make Mounds of Money, from an Expert Who Does it Every Day.

If you have an interest, look for it in bookstores, on the Web, or give my office a call at 800-262-1083 to learn more, or to order a copy. By the time you read this, our web site should be up at www.bestcfp.com. 888-TAX-WELL will get you to a free recorded message on my firm's services.

Anyway, professionally these days I practice financial planning, mostly in the areas of investment development and planning, and income and estate tax reduction strategies development. When people ask what I do, I say, "we save affluent people a ton in taxes - well beyond what their CPA and other advisors have been able to do." That pretty much sums it up. Making money through business or investment is great, and we are expert at showing our clients how better to do this. But it ain't what you make, it's what you get to keep, that counts. So shaving taxes to free up more for rein-vestment is the way to really put rocket fuel in wealth growth, and that's what we focus on.

There are so many ways...so many overlooked ways. Overlooked even by "rich" people with legions of advisors. We help those in need find them.

So that's what I do, when I'm not writing about cigars or messing with my kids, or my boats.

Told you it would be an unusual bio.

For those of you who prefer the more usual sort, here's one on me (written by who do you think?) that I've culled from a disclosure piece for one of my firms:

"Jeff Camarda has continued to serve the public in the financial field for well over a decade. Raised near New York City, he received his B.S. from the State University of New York in 1981, after earning his way through school by running his own antiques wholesale business. He became licensed as a full service stockbroker (series 7) in 1984, and led his 45-branch firm in production by 1986. Jeff obtained his general securities principal's license (series 24) in 1985, and managed brokerage branches in New York, Washington, DC, and Florida from 1986 through 1989.

Yearning to provide a more comprehensive, client-orientated level of service, in 1990 Jeff began study toward the Certified Financial Planner (CFP) professional designation. After two years of rigorous study and national examination, Jeff obtained certification in 1992, and immediately began work toward the Chartered Financial Consultant (ChFC) designation, a program similar to the CFP which he completed in 1994. His focused study of life insurance and related tax issues brought him the Chartered Life Underwriter (CLU) designation in early 1995, after which he began work toward a Ph.D. in finance, obtaining his degree (honors) in April of 1996. He is currently studying toward the Chartered Financial Analyst (CFA) designation, a demanding three-year program concentrating on economics, securities and markets analysis. At the time of this writing he is a CFA level II candidate, having passed the first of three annual examinations; no assurance can be given that the actual designation will be obtained.

A prolific writer, Jeff has been a frequent contributor to the Florida Times-Union (metro Jacksonville's dominant newspaper) and other area papers, writing about-weekly columns on investments, taxation, and personal finance for many years. His first book, **Wealth Health**, a comprehensive financial planning guide for the consumer based on his doctoral dissertation, is at this time being marketed by his literary agent. His second book is **The Sensible Cigar Connoisseur**. Wealth Health has been soundly endorsed by the Institute for Registered Financial Planners, and has been called "a great book, one of the finest books on financial planning yet written" by Fred Hills, Vice President of Simon & Schuster. Fred had gone so far as to say "I want to make it a national bestseller" - high praise from the editor responsible for the Charles Givens' "Wealth Without Risk" books, Jane Bryant Quinn's "Making the Most of Your Money," Peter Lynch's "Beating the Street" & "One Up on Wall Street," Robert Allen's "Nothing Down" books, "Louis Rukeyser's Business Almanac," as well as many other important bestsellers in the popular financial field. The cigar book has been endorsed by Lew Rothman, president and owner of J.R. Tobacco, the largest retailer and distributor of premium cigars in the world. Mr. Rothman has also been kind enough to provide a forward written by him for the cigar book. Jeff appeared weekly as a financial expert on the region's NBC affiliate's "Good Morning Jacksonville" (TLV-12) for several years, as well.

Passionate about his mission to help people attain financial security, Dr. Camarda is engaged in helping his clients to maximize their wealth and target their objectives through wealth management planning. He is the principal of J. Camarda & Associates, an independent vendor of high quality investment and insurance product from a variety of source institutions. It is recognized throughout metro-Jacksonville as one of the area's leading non-fee financial planning firms, and has as its clientele predominately area attorneys, physicians, and business owners.

Jeff is also president of Camarda Brothers, Financial Advisors, Inc., a fee-only planning firm.

Jeff practices what he preaches, investing effectively in the stock markets, and in Jacksonville-area real estate. He and wife Anne manage a personal real estate portfolio valued in excess of 5 million dollars through their company, Michaelangelo Property Management. At 40, their net worth approaches 4 million, built entirely "from scratch" by taking Jeff's tax and investment advice.

He is a member of Rotary, the Institute for Certified Financial Planners, the National Association of Life Underwriters, the United States Power Squadron, and has consistently qualified for membership in the Million Dollar Round Table.

Jeff makes his home in Orange Park, FL, with his wife Anne, and daughters Jennifer, Laurel, and J. Alexis. When not working, he enjoys boating, golf, fitness, writing, study, home projects, and family time, but notes that he is "a better boater than golfer," and vows to keep avoiding the game of golf by working on his boats."

[end third person bio]

Now tell me, which do you prefer?

Just to keep things straight, Fred and Simon & Schuster did not buy Wealth Health, mostly because of perceived problems associated with marketing an "unknown" (me). But when all's said, I bet they wished they had.

Well that's it on me, for now. I've included this piece to give some insight into the author for those readers who have an interest. When I really like a book, I know I do. I hope that you liked it, and laughed, and learned some useful things.

I loved writing it for you. I had a blast! Thanks for reading it.

Do I really have to go back to writing about estate planning and real estate now?

An Industry On Fire:
Cigar Sales And Growth Statistics

An Industry on Fire

Cigars are hot right now. They have never been hotter. After a long decline, the introduction of <u>Cigar Aficionado</u> in the early '90's spurred a resurgence of interest in cigars of incredible proportions. Stories about them abound in the media. The Internet is abuzz with them, sporting dedicated sites beyond count. Cigar clubs, smoker nights in major restaurants, and other events devoted to the passion abound. Major manufacturers bring their companies public for the first time in their long histories, and see their stock soar on huge waves of interest. Cigars grace the lips of celebrities like never before, and many of them, like Limbaugh, have become outspoken proponents. Supply is short, backorders are the norm, consumers can't get all they want despite more factories and acres planted with cigar tobacco then ever before in history. Smokers routinely pay $5, $10, even $50 for a single cigar, and count themselves lucky. Cigar smoke has become commonplace and accepted again in places like high-end clubs, restaurants, and hotels. Major magazines like <u>Cigar Aficionado</u> and <u>Smoke</u> see subscriptions surge, and find themselves thick and heavy with expensive advertising for high priced goods. The Web virtually pulses with cigar mania. Shops and mail order houses sprout everywhere. Hundreds of companies have cashed in on the craze and made their owners rich.

They will become richer still. New smokers have become legion. The cigar business is enjoying sustained double, even triple digit growth.

And the old smokers have come out of the closet.

They both tend to be affluent, passionate about the "hobby," and enthusiastic about spending well on related items. Thousands and more for a single desk-top humidor. Platinum and gold cigar cufflinks. Cutters, ashtrays, lighters and ties. Even books, like this one.

The cigar market is hot, indeed. Like most hobbies, its adherents are quite excited, and disposed to spending money on related things that they can pass time with.

The next section gives hard numbers on cigar sales and rates of increase, along with some pricing and smoker demographic data, and circulation data on Cigar Aficionado magazine. It finishes with some information on Wall Street's reaction to the trend. Articles and excerpts from which this data was have been obtained were "cut and pasted" from Internet sources.

National Cigar Sales Data

Through the late '80's and very early '90's, the premium cigar industry was mature, some would say dying. Sales were flat and they didn't seem to be making any more cigar smokers. The business was quite sleepy.

In 1991, however, a remarkable and unthinkable thing happened. Sales took off. Big time. And have continued at a accelerating pace since. Have a look at the graph below, showing that cigar sales in millions have nearly tripled over a five year period...despite annual price increases at double-digit rates.

This resurgence in demand is widely attributed to the appearance of <u>Cigar Aficionado</u> magazine, an upscale, gourmet-style bi-monthly which features cigars swathed between ads for Piaget watches and Gulfstream jets. It seemed to legitimize the hobby, to place premium cigars on a deserved pedestal far above the lowly, stinking stogie. But I think that the magazine catalyzed more than created the trend. I think that the market was ready to again embrace the gentle vice, as a very pleasant but not especially harmful indulgence. A complicated, rarefied, and somewhat mysterious pastime. Something to have fun with. A hobby to spend time with and learn more about.

The bulk of these new smokers are men in their 20's and 30's. And a surprising number of women have entered the fold.

For whatever reason, the trend is established. Beyond the explosive sales data, consider the fact that demand still far exceeds supply, and retailer's shelves are often half empty. Back-ordered product - unquenched demand - was estimated at 55 million units for the first half of 1996. Had the cigars been available, they would have sent the 1996 sales figure off the chart. Especially impressive, when one realizes that many cigars retailed at less that $2 in 1991 routinely fetched $10 in 1996. And still the market can't get enough. The growth rate is exponential. Makers and retailers ration their product to customers.

Cigars seem to be everywhere. In the hands of stars. Lots of stars. On the counters of supermarkets, convenience stores, gas stations, restaurants and bars. Liquor stores. Book stores. Lots of different stores, looking for add-on sales, looking to cash in on the trend. Not under the counter or in the back anymore, but right next to the register. Cigar-theme functions and cigar dinners occur very frequently in cities across the country.

And they are indeed everywhere. Just last night, my wife pointed out several cigar-related items offered in the Sugar Hill catalog, one of the many decorator circulars which line my mailbox each week. They have cigar candles at $89 the box of 25, Macanudo and sculpture cigar ashtrays, a cigar label lamp at $350, cigar cufflinks and "spirit holders," plus furniture, crystal, porcelain and pencil-boxes.

Cigar Aficionado Circulation Data

Although a host of cigar-dedicated periodicals - both paper and electronic - have appeared along with the wave of the cigar boom, <u>Cigar Aficionado</u> remains a premier publication, and has the longest history of circulation.

It's growth, like sales of the cigars themselves, has been extraordinary. Starting from zero in mid-1992, paid circulation had grown to 141,000 by winter of 1994. A year later, it had nearly doubled to 241,000. By winter of 1996, paid circulation was estimated at 380,000, with total readership in excess of 1,000,000. At that time, cigar sales were growing at a 60% per year clip and backorders were in the 80 million cigar range. Surely they have shot up even more since then. <u>Aficionado</u> had gone from quarterly to bi-monthly in that time, cigar stores, clubs, and -friendly restaurants continued to sprout, the World Wide Web has exploded with cigar sites, national weekly cigar radio programs have appeared.

And I haven't been able to get a single box of Punch or Hoyo de Monterry in all that time, despite a long standing and always current wholesale account with the manufacturer.

Please note that the circulation data above must be magnified by the now-myriad cigar periodicals, SMOKE magazine chief among them. If one counts the electronic delivery (try to get a number on that), total regular readership must be in the many millions by now.

Smokin' Stocks

Perhaps the best testimony that the above statistics point not to a fad but a long term trend comes from Wall Street. The number of cigar-making players who have, in the last year or so, for the first time in their mostly very long histories offered up stock in their companies to public investors, and in the investor's and analyst's reactions to the offerings.

Caribbean Cigar (OTC: CIGR) came out in August of '96, raising about $10 million for one-fifth of the company. The stock rose 62% on the first day of trading. The huge Consolidated Cigar (NY: CIG) sold $124 million in stock just a few weeks later, meeting so much demand that the initial "IPO" share price was set at a level well above the underwriting estimate. The same overwhelming demand met giant General Cigar's (NY: MPP) offering, which saw the $110 million worth of IPO shares leap 28% in value the first day. Huge and venerable Swisher International (NY: SWR) came out in December of '96. Also going public were Tamboril (OTC: SMKE) and The Ultimate Cigar Company (OTC: ULTC).

The above (for some companies, incomplete) data were obtained from Martin Luz's article "Putting Your Money Where Your Smokes Are," in the Summer '97 SMOKE Magazine. Mr. Luz goes on to say,

"But the real boom has been in the premium end of the market, which started taking off in 1991 and grew 68% last year alone. This is what has Wall Street all in a lather. 'The industry's fundamentals are extremely attractive,' says one portfolio manager...The 'fundamentals' he refers to are explosive growth in consumer demand and strong sales at every level (wholesale, retail, mail order - the whole enchilada); growing shortages and back orders; rising revenues and profits; expanding margins."

As I write this in midsummer of '97, JR Tobacco - the world's largest distributor and retailer of cigars and related products - is finalizing its own initial public offering through Prudential Securities. Go get 'em, Lew.

In summary of this section, let's review the annual growth data for "good" cigars, the kind the book is written about:

Year	Growth	Source	Rate Of Growth
1992	4%	Cigar Aficionado	BASE
1993	10%	Cigar Aficionado	150%
1994	12%	Cigar Aficionado	20%
1995	33%	Cigar Aficionado	175%
1996	59%	Cigar Aficionado projection	79%
1996	68%	SMOKE Magazine actual	106%

Even the numbers are smoking.

Where this trend will wind up is anyone's guess. If it matures like most, expect moderating growth to a peak, and eventual contraction as fashion changes and those who took up cigars merely because they were "in" move on to hang-glide polo or virtual dining or pet-part-piercing or whatever the next rage may be.

In its wake, however, look for a new, record-sized core of dedicated cigar smokers who stick with it. The baby boom is maturing, after all, and is the largest generation on record for the U.S. According to Rothman, past data show that cigar consumption peaks for smokers in their 50's. And for the baby boom, we're just getting close.

The cigar "fad," I think, will show a long and very bright afterglow.

Good smoke to all.

As an afterthought, don't be too awfully impressed by the cigar stock data presented above. It is meant to demonstrate consumer interest in the industry and in no way is a financial recommendation on my part. To invest, you need to peer a whole lot closer than that.

That's a whole 'nother area and a whole 'nother book to read. If you would like to read mine - which many have said is the best written on the subject - check out <u>Wealth Health</u>. At bookstores and other places. Or visit my sight at www.bestcfp.com, or call 888-TAX-WELL for free recorded information. Please forgive the plug, no pun intended!

The investment world has become an electronic jungle, though still rooted in the subways and basements of lower Manhattan. Be careful in there!

Index

A

accordion method 54
aging 138
  in the factory 139
agricultural and history buffs
  156
Airguide 134
all natural 47
Amaretto 191
amazon.com 159
Anchor Steam 189
antiques 147, 153
aquariums 142
Arturo Fuente 30, 34, 177
  Gran Reserva 63
  Hemingway 63
  Opus X 61
ashing 120
ashtrays 121, 145
assortment 185
atmosphere 96

B

baby boom 216
Baccarat 175
Bahamas 108
Bances 64, 174
Band Management 117
basic colors 74
Bass 189
Beck's 189
Becoming A Shrewd Smoker
  38
Beer 188
beetle 130

belicos 79
Belinda 55
big cigars 49
Big Smoke 107
binder 49, 71
binned 68
black marketeers 104
black-brown 75
blend 50, 72
blending 85
blending crops 52
blind tasting 58
blood nicotine levels 47
bogus boxes 105
book technique 53
Bordeaux 189
bottom-fishing 66
Bourbon 190
boyhood spitting skills 115
Brador 189
brand cigars 64
brand listings 158
Brazil 92
Bringing Cuban Cigars Into
  the U.S 109
British ales 189
bunching 51, 52, 72
Bundle Cigars 66
bundle deals 100
Burgundy 189
Burns, George 37, 39
butane 19, 116, 147
butchery 126
Buying Abroad 108

C

cabernets 189
cabinet box 153
café latte 188
cameroon wrapper 74
Canada 108
Canary Islands 92, 181
cap 112
capped 52
cappuccino 188
Caribbean Cigar (OTC: CIGR)
    215
Castro 57
cedar 141
cedar chests 141
Centro 60
Chablis 190
Chardonnay 190
check for draw 60
cheroots 49
chewers 45
Chiantis 189
China 92
Chinese mummies 48
chronometers 149
Churchill 60, 81
Cigar Aficionado
    33, 37, 44, 155, 211
  Buying Guide to Premium
    Cigars 58
  Subscription info 58
Cigar Anatomy 71
Cigar Band Museum - web site
    170
Cigar Books 156
Cigar Chic : A Woman's
    Perspective 180
cigar clubs 41, 106, 211
Cigar Companion, The
    67, 158
Cigar Connoisseur Radio
    Network 171
Cigar Construction 51
Cigar Cutters 112
Cigar Czar 157
cigar diameter 79
cigar dinners 158
Cigar Draw 59
Cigar Enthusiast, The 149
cigar filters 151
cigar holders 137
Cigar Insider 155
cigar makers 34
Cigar Manufacturers 33
Cigar Manufacturers Associa-
    tion 29
cigar market 212
cigar mold 52
cigar parts 126
Cigar Radio Network
    171, 172
Cigar Repairs 125
cigar sales 212
Cigar Scissors 113
Cigar Selection for Women
    180
cigar shortage 35
Cigar Smoking Tips for
    Women 180
cigar socks 149
cigar stock data 217
Cigar Virgins, The 30
Cigar-friendly 107
Cigar-Savor 145
cigarette smokers 46
Cigarillos 81, 83
Cigars ain't good for you 43
cigars and lifespans 44
cigars on the Internet 165
circulation data 212
Claro 76
Claro Claro or Candela 76
clear Havana 60

climate 39
Clipping the Head 112
Coffee 187
Cohibas 61, 105
collectibles 152, 153
Colorado 76
Colorado Claro 76
Colorado Maduro 76
colors 75
Columbia 93
Columbia University Cigar
    Society Links - web site
    168
complaints 123
concierge 108
conditions 133
Connecticut shade 77
Consolidated Cigar (NY: CIG)
    215
Cordials 191
Corona 81, 82
Corona Gorda 81
Corona Grande 81
corrugated technique 54
counterfeits 56, 88, 104
    bundles 106
countries 86
Credo 136
Cuba 87
Cuban cigars 31
Cuban coffee 187
Cuban customs officials 88
Cuban woman 38
Cubans 104
cuff links 149
culebras 79
cure 131
curly-head 52
Customs 110

D

Davidoff 31
diademas 81
diameter 79
dichotomy of brands 56
digital humidity meters 134
dimensions 77
dissect a cigar 54
distilled water 135
Dominican Republic
    29, 57, 89
Dominicans 67
Dominicans. 181
Don Diego 30, 34, 62
Don Mateo 68, 177
Don Thomas 62
Double Corona 81
double coronas 81
Draw 59
dress box 153
drink 187
drug store cigars 50
drugstore chains 67
Drugstores 101
dry cigar 131
Duty Free shops 32
duty free shops 108

E

Earth's Largest Bookstore 164
Ecuador 77
Edward's Pipe & Tobacco 15
El Rico 63
enjoy in moderation 48
entubar 53
escalating prices 29
espresso 188
Etiquette 122
European Market 31
Europe's premier cigar dealer

31
even lighting 183
evil trend 45
Excalibur 174
exchange flavor 139

F

Fakes 105
fashion 78
faux plug 126
Favorite Brands 173
Favorite Colors 178
Favorite Sizes 177
female content 179
fermentation 75
Fidel 57
figurados 79
filler leaf 72
filler leaves 71
filter 107
financial planning 204
fine restaurants 41
fingers 137
flint and steel 147
fold density 54
Frangelica 191
Fuente, Arturo. *See* Arturo
    Fuente
Fujipub.com Cigar Page - web
    site 169

G

G.G. Liddy 46
garbage 39
General Cigar's (NY: MPP)
    215
gigante 81
girth 80
Gran Reserva 177
Grand Marnier 191

green 75
Guillotine 112
guillotine 126
Guinness 189

H

H. Upman 30, 34, 56
Habana 56
Hacker 157
hand finished 55
hand made 55
handmade product 51
Havana cigars 32
health and pipe smokers 45
health safety tips 46
health studies 43
Hemmingway 177
Hencho a mano 55
higher prices 33
Hispanolia 89
Holders 150
Holt's 99
homogenated leaf 50
Honduran 39
Honduras 29, 57, 90
Hong Kong 108
How Cigars Are Rolled 52
How Long To Smoke 120
how to hold your cigar 183
Hoyo de Monterrey
    30, 56, 173
    Excalibur 61
humidifying agent 135
humidistatic devices 136
humidity 49, 133, 135
humidity gauges 134
humidor
    133, 135, 139, 140, 142
Humidors For The Truly
    Cheap 142
hyperspace 165

I

Ideal Conditions 133
Igor 120
InfoSeek 165
insects 130
Internet Cigar Group Web
   Site 168
Italy 108

J

J.R. Tobacco 67, 99
J.R. Ultimates 55, 174
Jamaica 29, 91, 181
jet flame 148
Jewelry 149
Joya de Nicaragua 62, 175
JR-CIGAR 15

K

Kennedy 56, 57
Kipling 37

L

La Gloria Cubana 69
ladies 179
Las Cabrillas 63
Leads From An Electronic
   Bookstore 159
leaks 75
Leaky Wrapper 128
Letterman 41
life insurance companies on
   cigar smoking 43
ligero 54, 72
light brown 75
lighters 147
Lighting 116, 183
liquor 188
Liquor stores 102

lockers 107
long ash 120, 121
long filler 49, 50
Lonsdale 81, 82
Lycos 165

M

Macanudo 62
machine bunched 55
machine rolled 55
made in Cuba 56
Madonna 41
Maduro 76, 181
Magazines 155
Mail Order Houses 98
major cigar producing countries 29
Man On The Street 104
Manhattan Special 191
manufacturers 33
marrying 139
matches 148
medium filler 51
meerschaum 150
Mexico 29, 91
microbrewery 189
Mineral water 187
mini course in cigar selection
   184
Mocha 67, 175
moderation 48
mold 135
Molsen 189
money clips 149
Montecruz 62
Mortality for cigar smokers 44

N

Nat Sherman 99
   Nat Sherman's A Passion

For Cigars 158
Natural or E.M.S 76
never inhale 46
new smokers 213
Nicaragua 29, 90
nicotine 181
   delivery system 47
   in cigars 46
   rush 47
Nino 56
non-Cuban counterfeits 106

O

oils 73, 139
Opus 177
organ donor 126
Oscuro 76
out of the country 108
overfilled 60, 126
ozone-generators 152

P

packaging 105
paid circulation 214
Panatela 81, 83
Paper matches 116
Partagas 55, 176
   1845 Limited Reserves 61
patches 75, 128
Paul Garmirian 63
perfecto 79
Petite Corona 81
Philippines 92
pilsners 189
pinot gregio 190
plugged cigar, repair 126
plugging 53
popularity of cigars 38
power cigar 63
premium cigar industry 212

Premium Cigars 63
private labels 32, 33
probe 125
puffing 118, 183
Punch 30, 56, 173
   Chateau 72
   Gran Cru 61, 174
punch, or drill 114
puro 91
Purpose Of This Book 38
Putting It Out 121
pyramid 79

Q

quarantine 130
quit once in awhile 48

R

Rave Reviews 15
reddish-brown 75
rehumidified cigar 131
rehydrate the mouth 190
relighting 119, 183
resilient 60
Riata 68
ring gauge 78, 79
rip-offs 34, 39
Robustos 63, 81, 82
Rothman, Lew 15, 29
Rothschilds 81, 82
Royal Jamaica 62
Rum 191
rye 190

S

Sabrosas 60
safest of the tobacco vices 45
sales data 213
Sam Adams 189
Sambuca 191

sandwich 51, 72
Scotch 190
sealing 75
search engines 166
seco 72
seconds 66
seegar 38
Selecting Cigars for Men 184
sexy 184
Shanken, Marvin 44, 155
shape 77
shirt studs 149
Shops 96
short filler 50
shortages 29, 39
shredding technique 122
shrewd smokers 38
Single malt 190
SMOKE 156
Smoke 211
Smoke Filters 151
smoke "green" 62
SMOKE-THIS 171
smoker demographic data 212
smoker nights 41, 211
Smoking Etiquette 122
smoking section 40, 122
smugglers 109
Soave 190
Sour Mash 190
sponge 135
spotting counterfeits 105
St. Pauli Girl 189
stock 211
storage conditions in shops 97
Strategies For A Tight Market
    102
Sumatra 77
sunspots 73
super premiums 30, 61
supply of cigars 35
Surgeon General's Report on

Smoking 44
Swisher International (NY:
    SWR) 215

T

Tamboril (OTC: SMKE) 215
tax seal 106
taxes in Canada 108
Te-Amo 62
Teasing Men with Your Cigar
    184
teeth 115
temperature 133
temporary storage 136
Thompson & Co 98
tie tacks 149
tobacco shops 185
Tobacco Village 17
Tobacconist Web Site 167
Tobacconists 95
too dry 134
too wet 134
Tools 125
toothy 73
torpedo 79
totalmente a machine 56
totmente a mano 55
toys 96
traditional tobacconists 34
traveling humidor 137
Tupperware 135, 142
Turkish coffee 188
Twain 37

U

U.S. "Cuban" supply 56
Ultimate Cigar Book, The 157
Ultimate Cigar Company
    (OTC: ULTC) 215
underfilled 60

Uneven Burn 128
unknown cigar brands 34
Unusual Shapes 79

V

V Cut 114
Varietals 190
vermeil 149
Villizon 61
vintage cigar 62
volado 72

W

Wall Street 214
water 135
Wealth Health 205
Web 165
webworm 165
Whiskey 190
why size matters 38
Winchester 49
windfall profits 30
Wine 189
winter 138
Women 179
wooden match 19, 116
workmanship 53
worms 129
   Hacker's cure 131
wrapper 73
   attributes 74
   leaf 52
www.bestcfp.com 206, 217
www.cc.columbia.edu./cu/
      cigar/links.html 168
www.cigaraficionado.com 166
www.cigargroup.com 168
www.mcs.net/~whizstrt/
      ciglinx.html 170
www.netins.net/showcase/

ORDER FORM
call 800.262.1083 to order now by credit card

FAX to   904-278-1070
MAIL to   Franklin Multimedia
           418 Kingsley Ave./ Orange Park, FL 32073

NAME:_____

ADDRESS:_____

PHONE: day_____evening_____

Price is $19.95 per book plus $2.95 shipping for up to three books.
(Additional shipping is $1 per book for over 3 books.)
Florida Residents please add 7% sales tax.

Books @ 19.95 _____

Shipping @ $2.95 _____

Additional shipping for each book
  over 3 at $1/book _____

TOTAL _____

Florida Residents add 7% Sales Tax _____

TOTAL including tax _____

Make Checks or Money Orders payable to:
Franklin Multimedia, Inc.

Credit Card Orders:
MC___VISA___Disc___AmEx___
Card Number:__ __ __ __-__ __ __ __-__ __ __ __-__ __ __ __
Exp. Date __ __-__ __

Name & Address of cardholder if different from above:
_____
I agree to the charges as described above.

Signature:_____

FAX A FRIEND

FAX TO: _____
@ Fax #   _____

You've got to check this out! This is the World's Best Cigar Book! It will make you a CIGAR MASTER! You'll LAUGH YOUR ASH OFF! NO KIDDING! Buy it! I loved it!

Regards, _____
(A delighted reader of <u>The Sensible Cigar Connoisseur</u>)

I Just Can't Wait Anymore!
Send me the World's Best Cigar Book NOW!

_ _

ORDER FORM
OR Call 800.262.1083 to order now by credit card

FAX: 904-278-1070   OR   MAIL: Franklin Multimedia
                                    418 Kingsley Ave
                                    Orange Park, FL 32073

NAME:_____
ADDRESS:_____
PHONE: day_____evening_____
Price is $19.95 per book plus $2.95 shipping for up to three books.
(Additional shipping is $1 per book for over 3 books.)

Books @ 19.95   _____
Shipping @ $2.95   _____
Additional shipping for each book
   over 3 at $1/book   _____
TOTAL   _____
Florida Residents add 7% Sales Tax   _____

TOTAL including tax   _____

Make Checks or Money Orders payable to: Franklin Multimedia, Inc.

Credit Card Orders:
MC___VISA___Disc___AmEx___
Card Number:_ _ _ _-_ _ _ _-_ _ _ _-_ _ _ _ Exp. _ _-_ _
Name & Address of cardholder if different from above:
_____
I agree to the charges as described above.

Signature: _____